GROUNDWORK FOR A BETTER VOCABULARY

D0885315

Instructor's Edition

R. Kent Smith

UNIVERSITY OF MAINE

Carole Mohr

TOWNSEND PRESS Marlton, NJ 08053

The Seven Books in the Townsend Press Vocabulary Series:

GROUNDWORK FOR A BETTER VOCABULARY
BUILDING VOCABULARY SKILLS
IMPROVING VOCABULARY SKILLS
ADVANCING VOCABULARY SKILLS
BUILDING VOCABULARY SKILLS, SHORT VERSION
IMPROVING VOCABULARY SKILLS, SHORT VERSION
ADVANCING VOCABULARY SKILLS, SHORT VERSION

Supplements Available for Each Book:

Instructor's Manual and Test Bank
Set of Computer Disks

For information on any of these books or supplements,
or other books on the Townsend Press reading list,
write to the address shown below.

Townsend Press, Inc.
Pavilions at Greentree—408
Marlton, New Jersey 08053
609-772-6410

Send books orders and requests for desk copies or supplements to:

Townsend Press Book Center
RD # 11, Box 192A
Mt. Penn Road
Reading, PA 19607
1-215-796-0929
FAX 1-215-796-1491

ISBN 0-944210-84-8

PE 1449
.S62527

Contents

Note: For ease of reference, the title of the passage that concludes each chapter appears in parentheses.

UNIT FOUR

UNIT FIVE

Appendixes

Preface

The problem is all too familiar: *students just don't know enough words*. Reading, writing, and content teachers agree that many students' vocabularies are inadequate to the demands of courses. Weak vocabularies limit students' understanding of what they read and the clarity and depth of what they write.

The purpose of the Townsend Press vocabulary series is to provide a solid, workable answer to the vocabulary problem. GROUNDWORK FOR A BETTER VOCABULARY, the first book in the series, teaches 150 important basic words. It contains thirty chapters, with five words in each chapter. Here are the distinctive features of the text:

1 An intensive words-in-context approach. Studies show that students learn words best by seeing them repeatedly in different contexts, not through rote memorization. GROUNDWORK FOR A BETTER VOCABULARY gives students an intensive in-context experience by presenting each word in at least six different contexts. Each chapter takes students through a productive sequence of steps:

- Students first see a word in a preview.
- They then infer the meaning of the word by considering two sentences in which it appears.
- Based on their inferences, students select and confirm each word's meaning in a matching test. They are then in a solid position to further deepen their knowledge of a word.
- Finally, they strengthen their understanding and memory of each word by applying it in four practices. In the first two practices, words appear in sentence contexts; in the third practice, students work with synonyms, antonyms, and word parts; in the final practice, words appear in the context of an entire passage.

Every encounter with a word brings it closer to becoming part of the student's permanent word bank.

2 Abundant practice. In addition to the extensive practice in each chapter, there are *two unit tests* at the end of each six-chapter unit. These tests reinforce students' knowledge of every word in every chapter. Further, there are added tests in the *Test Bank* and on the *computer disks* that accompany the book. All this practice means that students learn in the surest possible way: by working closely and repeatedly with each word.

3 Continuing reinforcement. To provide even more review, most of the words in each chapter are repeated in context in later chapters of the book. Repeated words are marked with underlines.

4 Controlled feedback. Students receive immediate feedback on two of the practices in each vocabulary chapter. A limited answer key at the back of the book lets them see how they did with the opening preview of words. The key also provides answers for the first sentence practice in the chapter. The key enables students to take an active role in their own learning. They are likely to use this answer key in an honest and positive way if they know they may be tested on the many activities for which answers are not provided. (Answers to all the practices in the student book are in the *Instructor's Edition*. They can, of course, be copied from the IE and passed out at the teacher's discretion.)

5 Focus on essential words. A good deal of time and research went into selecting the 150 words featured in the book. Word frequency lists were consulted, along with lists in a wide number of vocabulary books. In addition, the authors and editors each prepared their own lists. A computer was used to help in the consolidation of the many word lists. A long process of group discussion then led to final decisions about the words that would be most helpful for students on a basic reading level.

6 Appealing content. Dull practice materials work against learning. On the other hand, meaningful, lively, and at times even funny sentences and passages can spark students' attention and thus encourage their grasp of the material. For this reason, a great deal of effort was put into creating sentences and passages with both widespread appeal *and* solid context support. We have tried throughout to make the practice materials truly enjoyable for teachers and students alike. Look, for example, at the passage on page 8 that closes the first chapter of this book.

7 Clarity of format. The book has been designed so that its very format contributes to the learning process. The "Five Words in Context" and the matching test are on the same page, making it easy for students to visually "travel" between the sentences and the definitions as they try to determine a word's meaning from the sentence contexts. Also, a second color has been used within the book to help make the content as visually appealing as possible.

8 Supplementary materials.

a A combined *Instructor's Manual and Test Bank* is available at no charge to instructors using the book. It can be obtained by writing to the Reading Editor, Townsend Press, Pavilions at Greentree—408, Marlton, NJ 08053. This booklet contains a pretest and posttest for the words in the text as well as teaching suggestions, a model syllabus, mastery tests for each chapter, and an answer key.

b A *vocabulary test kit* is also provided without charge to instructors using the book. The kit consists of a pretest and posttest for all 150 words in the book as well as answer sheets and an answer key. Upon request, as many copies of the test booklets will be sent as there are students using the book. With the help of the booklets, a teacher can easily test students' knowledge of the 150 words at the start of the semester and then retest at the end of the semester, to measure exactly how much each student has improved.

c A *series of computer disks* also accompanies the book. These disks provide two tests for each of the thirty vocabulary chapters. The disks are self-loading and contain a number of other user- and instructor-friendly features: explanations of answers, a sound option, mention of the user's first name, a score at the bottom of the screen, and a record-keeping file.

Probably in no other area of reading instruction is the computer more useful than in reinforcing vocabulary. This vocabulary program takes advantage of the computer's unique capabilities and motivational appeal. Here's how the program works:

- Students are tested on the five words in a chapter, with each word in a sentence context different from any in the book itself.
- After students answer each question, they receive immediate feedback: The computer tells if a student is right or wrong and *why*, frequently using the student's first name and providing a running score.
- When the test is over, the computer supplies a test score.

By the end of this program, students' knowledge of each word in the chapter will have been carefully reinforced. And this reinforcement will be the more effective for having occurred in an electronic medium that especially engages today's students.

A demo disk will be sent to any teacher requesting it. The set of disks, with unlimited copying privileges, will be available at no charge to departments adopting at least fifty copies of the book.

9 Realistic pricing. We wanted a book that would offer the highest possible quality at the best possible price. We are delighted that Townsend Press has committed to sell this book at a price of less than ten dollars. Such a modest charge makes it an inexpensive supplement for any reading or writing course.

10 One in a sequence of books. GROUNDWORK FOR A BETTER VOCABULARY is the basic book in the Townsend Press Vocabulary Series. The other books in the series are BUILDING VOCABULARY SKILLS, IMPROVING VOCABULARY SKILLS, and ADVANCING VOCABULARY SKILLS; there are also short versions of these three books. Suggested grade levels for each book are included in the *Instructor's Manual*. GROUNDWORK FOR A BETTER VOCABULARY and either of the sets of three books will help create a vocabulary foundation that will make any student a better reader, writer, and thinker.

Acknowledgments

Our thanks go to the talented group of writers and editors at Townsend Press who have worked closely with us on the book: John Langan, Beth Johnson Ruth, and Jane Mackay. We also acknowledge the programming efforts of Professor Terry Hutchison of Atlantic Community College. He has helped us create the kind of user-friendly software that we believe can really help solidify students' learning of all the words in the book. Inspiration for the cover came from an idea by Janet M. Goldstein, and the cover itself owes thanks to the artistry of Larry Didona. We appreciate as well the page design work of Alysse Einbender and Patty Mayer, and we are particularly grateful for the design, editing, and proofreading skills of Janet M. Goldstein.

R. Kent Smith   *Carole Mohr*

Introduction

WHY VOCABULARY DEVELOPMENT COUNTS

You have probably often heard it said, "Building vocabulary is important." Maybe you've politely nodded in agreement and then forgotten the matter. But it would be fair for you to ask, "Why *is* vocabulary development important? Provide some proof." Here are four strong pieces of evidence.

1   Common sense tells you what many research studies have shown as well: vocabulary is a basic part of becoming a better reader. Simply put, if you don't know enough words, you are going to have trouble understanding what you read. An occasional word may not stop you, but if there are too many words you don't know, your reading will suffer. The *content* of textbooks is often challenge enough; you don't want to work as well on understanding the *words* that make up that content.

2   Vocabulary is a major part of almost every standardized test, including reading achievement tests, college entrance exams, and armed forces and vocational placement tests. Test authors know that vocabulary is a key measure of both one's learning and one's ability to learn, so they include a separate vocabulary section in their tests. The more words you know, then, the better you are likely to do on such important tests.

3   Studies have made clear that students with strong vocabularies are more successful in school. And one widely known study found that a good vocabulary, more than any other factor, was common to people enjoying successful careers in life. Words are in fact the tools not just of better reading, but of writing, speaking, listening, and thinking as well. The more words you have at your command, the more effective your communication can be, and the more influence you can have on the people around you.

4   In the world of the 1990s, a good vocabulary will count more than ever. Far fewer people will work on farms or in factories. Far more will be in jobs that provide services or process information. More than ever, words will be the tools of our trade: words we use in reading, writing, listening, and speaking. In addition, experts say that workers of the 90s will be called on to change jobs and learn new skills at an ever-increasing pace. The keys to survival and success will thus be the abilities to communicate skillfully and learn quickly. A solid vocabulary is essential for both of these skills.

The evidence is great, then, that building vocabulary is very important for growth and success. The question then becomes, "What is the best way of going about it?"

WORDS IN CONTEXT: THE KEY TO VOCABULARY DEVELOPMENT

Memorizing lists of words is a traditional method of vocabulary development. But a person is likely to forget such memorized lists quickly. Studies show that to master a word you must see and use it in various contexts. By working actively and repeatedly with a word, you greatly increase the chance of really learning it.

The following activity will make clear how the book is organized and how it uses a words-in-context approach. Answer the questions or fill in the missing words in the spaces provided.

Contents

Turn to the table of contents on pages iii-iv.

• How many chapters are in the book? _____*30*_____

• Three short sections follow the chapters. The first provides a **limited answer key**; the

   second gives helpful information on using _____*a dictionary*_____; and the third is

   an **index** of the 150 words in the book.

Vocabulary Chapters

Turn to Chapter 1 on pages 5-8. This chapter, like all the others, consists of seven parts:

• The **first part**, on page 5, is titled _____*Previewing the Words*_____

This preview introduces you to the five words covered in the chapter. After you try filling in the blanks, you are asked to check the _____*answers*_____ at the back and to fill in any empty blanks.

• The **second part** of the chapter, on page 6, is titled _____*Five Words in Context*_____

The left-hand column lists the five words. Under each word is its _____*pronunciation*_____ (in parentheses) and its part of speech (*noun, verb,* or *adjective*). For example, we are told that *communicate,* the first word on page 6, is a verb.

Using the pronunciation guide requires only a bit of information: Short vowels have no special mark, while long vowels are shown with a line above the vowel. (Note that long vowels have the sound of their own name.) What is the first word in the list with a long

vowel? _____*communicate*_____ . Symbols that have an unaccented sound, like the *a* in *about* or the *e* in *item,* are shown by the schwa (ə), which looks like an upside down *e.*

What is the first word in the list with a schwa? _____*communicate*_____. Finally, an accent mark (') tells which syllable to accent when pronouncing a word. What is the first

word in the list with an accent on the second syllable? _____*communicate*_____ A brief guide to the dictionary on pages 149-151 gives further information on pronouncing words.

To the right of each word are two sentences that help you understand its meaning. In each sentence, the *context*—the words surrounding the boldfaced word—provides clues you can use to figure out the definition. For example, look at the first sentence for the word *deceive*:

Jason **deceived** Linda. He dated her without telling her he was married.

Based on the context, what is the meaning of *deceive*?

    a. meet   (b.) mislead   c. help   d. like

A second sentence also helps you pin down the meaning:

A business person who tries to **deceive** customers should be reported to the Better Business Bureau.

By looking closely at each pair of sentences, you can decide on the meaning of a word. (In the examples above, *deceive* clearly means *mislead*.) As you figure out each meaning, you are working actively with the word. You are creating the groundwork you need to understand *and* to remember the word. Getting involved with the word and developing a feel for it, based upon its use in context, is the key to word mastery.

It is with good reason, then, that the directions at the top of page 6 tell you to look

_____ *closely* _____ and _____ *carefully* _____ at the context. Doing so deepens your sense of the word and prepares you for the next activity.

• The ***third part*** of the chapter, at the bottom of page 6, is titled _____

_____ *Matching Words and Definitions* _____.

According to research, it is not enough to see a word in context. At a certain point, it is important as well to see the meaning of a word. The matching test provides that meaning, but it also makes you look for and think about that meaning. In other words, it continues the active learning that is your surest route to learning and remembering a word.

Your work throughout the chapter will depend on the accuracy of your answers to this test. Do not go any further, then, until you are sure that your answers are correct.

• The ***fourth part*** of the chapter, on page 7, is titled _____ *Check 1* _____.

This practice helps you to firm up your understanding of the five words and helps you notice when words have more than one meaning. (Many words have more than one meaning. For example, *see* can mean "to notice with the eyes"—"I see the bus"—or "to understand"—"I see what you mean.") After filling in the blanks for this activity, check your answers in the limited key at the back of the book. Be sure to use the answer key as a learning tool only. Doing so will help you to master the words and to prepare for the last two activities and the unit tests, for which answers are not provided.

• The *fifth part* of the chapter, also on page 7, is titled _____ *Check 2* _____ , and the *sixth part*, at the top of page 8, is titled _____ *Check 3* _____ .

Both of these practices test you on all five words, giving you a chance to deepen your mastery. The sixth activity varies from chapter to chapter.

• At the bottom of page 8 is the *seventh part* of the chapter, titled _____ *Final Check* _____ . In this activity, you have the context of an entire passage in which you can practice and apply the words.

Following the final practice is a box where you can enter your score for the final three checks. These scores should also be entered into the vocabulary performance chart located on the inside back page of the book.

You now know, in a nutshell, how to work with the activities in each chapter. Make sure that you do each page very carefully. *Remember, as you work through the activities, you are learning the words.*

How many times in all will you use each word? If you look, you'll see that each chapter gives you the opportunity to work with each word eight times. Each contact with a word increases the chance that the word will become part of your active vocabulary.

You will have further opportunities to use each word in the two unit tests that follow each unit and on the computer disks that are available with the book. Finally, to provide even more review, most of the words in each chapter are repeated in context in later chapters of the book. Repeated words are marked with underlines.

FINAL THOUGHTS

The facts are in. A strong vocabulary is a source of power. Words can make you a better reader, writer, speaker, thinker, and learner. They can greatly increase your chances of success in school and in your job.

But words will not come without effort. They must be learned in a program of regular study. If you commit yourself to learning words, and you work actively and honestly with the chapters in this book, you will not only enrich your vocabulary—you will enrich your life as well.

Unit One

Previewing the Words

Find out how many of the five words in this chapter you already know. Try to complete each sentence with the most suitable word from the list below. Use each word once.

Leave a sentence blank rather than guessing at an answer. Your purpose here is just to get a sense of the five words and what you may know about them.

communicate	deceive	earnest
fiction	theory	

1. Charlotte's sweet smiles don't _____*deceive*_____ me. I know she really dislikes me.

2. Dolphins _____*communicate*_____ with one another through a language of squeaks and grunts.

3. When I want to relax, I read love stories, mysteries, and other kinds of _____*fiction*_____.

4. Murphy has a(n) _____*theory*_____ about life. He believes that everything that can possibly go wrong, will.

5. When George begged his boss for another chance, he seemed so _____*earnest*_____ that his employer decided to give him his job back.

Now check your answers by turning to page 145. Fix any mistakes and fill in any blank spaces by writing in the correct answers. By doing so, you will complete this introduction to the five words.

You're now ready to strengthen your knowledge of the words you already know and to master the words you're only half sure of, or don't know at all. Turn to the next page.

Five Words in Context

Figure out the meanings of the following five words by looking *closely and carefully* at the sentences below. Doing so will prepare you for the matching test and practices that follow.

1 **communicate**
(kə-myōō'-nə-kāt')
-*verb*

   a. Alice and I rarely see each other, but we **communicate** often with letters and phone calls.

   b. The storm had knocked down their telephone lines, so the Bakers had no way to **communicate** their need for a doctor.

2 **deceive**
(di-sēv')
-*verb*

   a. Jason **deceived** Linda. He dated her without telling her he was married.

   b. A business person who tries to **deceive** customers should be reported to the Better Business Bureau.

3 **earnest**
(ûr'-nĭst)
-*adjective*

   a. My brother's fear of bees is **earnest**. He's not kidding when he says a bee bite can kill him.

   b. Jimmy seemed **earnest** when he promised to clean the windows by Friday, so I was surprised to see he hadn't done them.

4 **fiction**
(fĭk'-shən)
-*noun*

   a. One of the most amusing pieces of **fiction** is Mark Twain's story of a Connecticut man who traveled back to the time of King Arthur's Court.

   b. Some papers print obvious **fiction**, such as "Nine-year-old girl has triplets who weigh 100 pounds more than she does!!!"

5 **theory**
(thē'-ə-rē)
-*noun*

   a. According to the **theory** of evolution, the environment affects how animals and plants develop over the centuries.

   b. The police's **theory** was that the killer was a short man with dark hair, but the murderer turned out to be a blond woman wearing a dark wig.

Matching Words and Definitions

Check your understanding of the five words by matching each word with its definition. The sentences above will help you decide on the meaning of each word.

   b   1. **communicate**   a. literature consisting of imaginary stories; anything made up

   e   2. **deceive**   b. to exchange or give information or thoughts; to make known

   d   3. **earnest**   c. a statement of the system behind events or facts; an unproven explanation; a guess

   a   4. **fiction**   d. seriously important; serious and sincere

   c   5. **theory**   e. to make (someone) believe what is not true

➤ Check 1

Complete each sentence below with the correct word from the box. Use each word once.

communicate	deceive	earnest
fiction	theory	

1. Language isn't the only way to _____*communicate*_____. Facial expressions and body movements can also give us information.
2. If you make someone believe a lie, you have _____*deceive*_____d that person.
3. We try to make sense of facts by thinking of a general _____*theory*_____ to explain them.
4. "_____*Fiction*_____" has several meanings, but they all refer to made-up ideas.
5. The word "_____*earnest*_____" can describe something (for example, a feeling or statement) that is serious and important or someone who is very sincere.

Now check your answers to these questions by turning to page 145. Going over the answers carefully will help you prepare for the next three practices, for which answers are not given.

➤ Check 2

Complete each sentence below with the correct word from the box. Use each word once.

communicate	deceive	earnest
fiction	theory	

1. Please _____*communicate*_____ my congratulations to Dominic.
2. Every explanation of how the Earth began is an unproven _____*theory*_____.
3. Don't let the ad for diet pills _____*deceive*_____ you—losing weight isn't so easy.
4. Our club has a(n) _____*earnest*_____ concern for the poor, so we decided to pass out warm jackets to homeless people.
5. Just because _____*fiction*_____ is made up doesn't mean it has nothing important to say. Novels, short stories, and poetry can teach us a lot.

➤ *Check 3*

Circle the letter of the best answer to each question.

1. A person can *communicate*   a. a building   (b.) an idea   c. a garden
2. *Deceive* means the **same** as   a. encourage   b. hit   (c.) mislead
3. The **opposite** of *earnest* is   (a.) insincere   b. late   c. wrong
4. The **opposite** of *fiction* is   a. story   (b.) facts   c. names
5. An important purpose of *theories* is to   a. puzzle   b. deny   (c.) explain

➤ *Final Check:* **Children's Lies**

Read the following passage carefully. Then fill in each blank with a different word from the box. (Context clues will help you figure out which word goes in which blank.)

communicate	deceive	earnest
fiction	theory	

Some people think children are "born liars" who enjoy telling untrue stories just to (1)_____*deceive*_____ others. I disagree. Although I have no scientific proof, my (2)_____*theory*_____ is that children mix (3)_____*fiction*_____ in with their facts for some very good reasons. For example, a child may miss her father and want some special attention from him. He usually says he's too busy when she (4)_____*communicate*__s a desire to play with him or to have him read her a story. So she makes up something more attention-grabbing, such as "There's a tiger under my bed." If we listen carefully to the "lies" a child tells, we may find they are really about (5)_____*earnest*_____ needs that are not being met.

SCORES: Check 2 _____ %   Check 3 _____ %   **Final Check** _____ %

2

Previewing the Words

Find out how many of the five words in this chapter you already know. Try to complete each sentence with the most suitable word from the list below. Use each word once.

Leave a sentence blank rather than guessing at an answer. Your purpose here is just to get a sense of the five words and what you may know about them.

appropriate	**bewilder**	**emotion**
investigate	**legible**	

1. Do you believe the <u>theory</u>* that love is the most powerful _____*emotion*_____?

2. At first, the numerous noises, flashing lights, and whirling rides of the fair

   _____*bewilder*_____(e)d the children.

3. When we go on our walks, my dog _____*investigate*_____s every bush and tree we come across.

4. At the fancy dinner, Sheila watched her hostess to see which fork was

   _____*appropriate*_____ for each course.

5. Ten years ago, I carved my initials in a tree. Recently I was surprised to see that

   they were still _____*legible*_____.

   *Words from previous chapters are underlined throughout the book. Words are repeated to give you more chance for review and mastery.

Now check your answers by turning to page 145. Fix any mistakes and fill in any blank spaces by writing in the correct answers. By doing so, you will complete this introduction to the five words.

You're now ready to strengthen your knowledge of the words you already know and to master the words you're only half sure of, or don't know at all. Turn to the next page.

Five Words in Context

Figure out the meanings of the following five words by looking *closely and carefully* at the sentences below. Doing so will prepare you for the matching test and practices that follow.

1 **appropriate**
(ə-prō'-prē-it)
-*adjective*

a. While it's **appropriate** to scream one's approval at a football game, such behavior is not considered proper at the ballet.

b. Walking shoes aren't **appropriate** for jogging.

2 **bewilder**
(bi-wil'-dər)
-*verb*

a. The large new school at first **bewildered** Chung, but after a day or two, getting around was no longer confusing to him.

b. My grandmother's poor health **bewildered** the doctor until he found out she wasn't taking her medicines.

3 **emotion**
(i-mō'-shən)
-*noun*

a. Many people have trouble talking about their **emotions,** especially their anger and fear.

b. Stan rarely showed his **emotions**. We had to guess what he was really feeling.

4 **investigate**
(in-ves'-tə-gāt')
-*verb*

a. The FBI has been called in to **investigate** the disappearance of the baby from the hospital.

b. When I heard a noise downstairs at 3 a.m., I lay still in bed, too frightened to get up and **investigate** the situation.

5 **legible**
(lej'-ə-bəl)
-*adjective*

a. My father used to make me rewrite my sloppy homework. "I can barely read this," he'd say. "Make it **legible**."

b. The fancy script on that new restaurant sign isn't fully **legible**. Does it say "Peretti's," "Perelli's," or "Pepelli's"?

Matching Words and Definitions

Check your understanding of the five words by matching each word with its definition. The sentences above will help you decide on the meaning of each word.

_d_	1. **appropriate**	a.	to confuse; puzzle
_a_	2. **bewilder**	b.	a feeling
_b_	3. **emotion**	c.	able to be read
_e_	4. **investigate**	d.	proper; suited to a certain use or purpose
_c_	5. **legible**	e.	to explore or examine carefully, in order to learn the facts

➤*Check 1*

Complete each sentence below with the correct word from the box. Use each word once.

appropriate	bewilder	emotion
investigate	legible	

1. Love and hate are opposite _____*emotion*_____s.

2. A large school with many hallways is bound to _____*bewilder*_____ a new student.

3. A message that's badly scribbled may not be _____*legible*_____.

4. It's a detective's job to _____*investigate*_____ crimes.

5. Running shoes are more _____*appropriate*_____ for jogging than walking shoes because they protect a runner's foot better.

Now check your answers to these questions by turning to page 145. Going over the answers carefully will help you prepare for the next three practices, for which answers are not given.

➤*Check 2*

Complete each sentence below with the correct word from the box. Use each word once.

appropriate	bewilder	emotion
investigate	legible	

1. Arnie has neat, clear handwriting. I wish mine were so _____*legible*_____.

2. After sitting in unmoving traffic for twenty minutes, Dad ran ahead to _____*investigate*_____ the cause of the delay.

3. At first, Kwan showed no _____*emotion*_____ when she was given the award—her face was blank.

4. My sister was sent home from junior high school to change her clothes. Her teacher said miniskirts were not _____*appropriate*_____ at school.

5. Receiving a card signed with an unfamiliar name _____*bewilder*_____(e)d me until I realized it was sent by an old girlfriend who had gotten married.

➤Check 3

Circle the letter of the best answer to each question.

1. *Appropriate* means the opposite of   a. successful (b.)improper   c. difficult

2. Someone who *investigates* a situation   a. avoids it   b. causes it   (c.)explores it

3. Stories meant to *bewilder* us are called (a.)mysteries   b. comedies   c. romances

4. An *emotion* is something we   a. marry   b. taste   (c.)feel

5. To create *legible* words, practice your   a. grammar   b. pronunciation (c.)handwriting

➤*Final Check:* A Mysterious Letter

Read the following passage carefully. Then fill in each blank with a different word from the box. (Context clues will help you figure out which word goes in which blank.)

appropriate	bewilder	emotion
investigate	legible	

   The saying that truth is stranger than <u>fiction</u> has been proved by my roommate Andy's experience. Last Thursday, Andy received a letter that has completely (1)_____*bewilder*_____(e)d him. He isn't confused about what it says—it's clearly typed and thus quite (2)_____*legible*_____. What he's confused about is who it is from. You see, our puppy got a hold of it while it was still in the envelope and chewed up a corner—the corner the signature was on. It's clear the letter is from one of Andy's female friends from his hometown, but he has no idea which one.

   He's going crazy wondering who the letter is from because it's about a very important (3)_____*emotion*_____: love. Basically, the letter says, "You and I have always been good friends, but I have to tell you that my feelings for you have grown into more than friendship."

   Poor Andy isn't quite sure what to do. In order to (4)_____*investigate*_____ the mystery, he'll go home next month and visit all the girls he knows. Once he discovers who his "mystery love" is, he'll be able to decide what he wants to <u>communicate</u> to her in return. He wonders which response will be most (5)_____*appropriate*_____: "Thanks, but no thanks"? "Let's give it a try"? Or "How could I be so lucky"?

SCORES:	Check 2 _____ %	Check 3 _____ %	Final Check _____ %

Enter your scores above and in the vocabulary performance chart on the inside back cover of the book.

Previewing the Words

Find out how many of the five words in this chapter you already know. Try to complete each sentence with the most suitable word from the list below. Use each word once.

Leave a sentence blank rather than guessing at an answer. Your purpose here is just to get a sense of the five words and what you may know about them.

burden	**economical**	**extravagant**
security	**sympathize**	

1. We'd love to go to Disney World this year, but we're low on money. We'll have to

   plan a more _____*economical*_____ vacation.

2. The hospital guards provide _____*security*_____ for staff and patients.

3. I show that I _____*sympathize*_____ when a friend's relative dies by sending a memorial donation to a charity.

4. Warren has no brothers or sisters, so he has the entire _____*burden*_____ of caring for his sick, elderly mother.

5. When my sister told her boyfriend that it was _____*extravagant*_____ to spend as much as he did on dinner and a show, he said, "But nothing is too good for you, darling."

Now check your answers by turning to page 145. Fix any mistakes and fill in any blank spaces by writing in the correct answers. By doing so, you will complete this introduction to the five words.

You're now ready to strengthen your knowledge of the words you already know and to master the words you're only half sure of, or don't know at all. Turn to the next page.

Five Words in Context

Figure out the meanings of the following five words by looking *closely and carefully* at the sentences below. Doing so will prepare you for the matching test and practices that follow.

1 **burden**
(bûr'-dn)
-noun

   a. Although others think raising a handicapped child must be a **burden**, my neighbor says she has found joy, not hardship, in caring for her son.

   b. At first, stealing the money didn't bother Annie. But in time, her crime became a great **burden**.

2 **economical**
(ē'-kə-nom'-i-kəl)
-adjective

   a. It's usually more **economical** to buy food and soap in large packages, but sometimes the smaller package costs less per ounce.

   b. To decide which car is most **economical**, compare prices, gas mileage and repair costs.

3 **extravagant**
(ik-strav'-ə-gənt)
-adjective

   a. Since I considered it **extravagant** to buy a prom dress that I'd wear only once, I borrowed one from a friend.

   b. Rhoda is on such a tight budget that she felt it was wildly **extravagant** to buy herself a ten-dollar pair of earrings.

4 **security**
(si-kyoor'-i-tē)
-noun

   a. For nighttime **security**, the owner of the jewelry shop turns on a burglar alarm.

   b. It's considered <u>appropriate</u> for a 2-year-old to carry a blanket for **security**, but it's thought odd if a 12-year-old calms his fears in that way.

5 **sympathize**
(sim'-pə-thīz')
-verb

   a. I **sympathize** with Betty's disappointment at her family forgetting her birthday. The same thing happened to me last year.

   b. To show he **sympathized** with Mrs. Owen when her husband died, Scott sent her flowers and a card.

Matching Words and Definitions

Check your understanding of the five words by matching each word with its definition. The sentences above will help you decide on the meaning of each word.

_c_   1. **burden**   a. spending no more than necessary; thrifty

_a_   2. **economical**   b. protection; freedom from danger, fear, or worry

_e_   3. **extravagant**   c. a hardship; something difficult to bear

_b_   4. **security**   d. to understand or share in another's feelings or ideas; to feel sorrow for another's trouble or suffering

_d_   5. **sympathize**   e. spending much more than is necessary or wise; wasteful

➤ *Check 1*

Complete each sentence below with the correct word from the box. Use each word once.

burden	economical	extravagant
security	sympathize	

1. After people are robbed, they often feel a greater need for _____ *security* _____ .

2. A _____ *burden* _____ may be a physical or a mental hardship, or both.

3. An _____ *economical* _____ person doesn't like to waste money.

4. An _____ *extravagant* _____ person enjoys spending a lot of money.

5. It's easier to _____ *sympathize* _____ with someone's feelings when we've had the same difficult experience that he or she has had.

Now check your answers to these questions by turning to page 145. Going over the answers carefully will help you prepare for the next three practices, for which answers are not given.

➤ *Check 2*

Complete each sentence below with the correct word from the box. Use each word once.

burden	economical	extravagant
security	sympathize	

1. When strangers are around, our cat finds _____ *security* _____ under the sofa.

2. It's not _____ *economical* _____ to buy large packages of food if much of the food spoils before you get around to eating it.

3. I _____ *sympathize* _____ with the young man whose new car was dented in the parking lot. The same thing happened to my first car.

4. I'm usually thrifty, but when I got a big raise last year, I decided to be
_____ *extravagant* _____ and take a trip to England.

5. After Mrs. Ryan fainted, her children learned that she'd been ill for weeks, but hadn't
wanted to be a _____ *burden* _____ to them.

➤Check 3

Circle **C** if the italicized word is used **correctly**, Circle **I** if the word is used **incorrectly**.

Ⓒ I   1. Many people think of taxes as a *burden*.

C Ⓘ   2. All the muggings in our neighborhood have given us a strong feeling of *security*.

Ⓒ I   3. For a more *economical* holiday season, make some of your gifts instead of buying them all.

C Ⓘ   4. My boyfriend thought I was too *extravagant* when I bought a used car instead of a new one.

Ⓒ I   5. Barry's parents did not *sympathize* with his disappointment over his low grades because they felt the grades were Barry's own fault.

➤Final Check: Differing Attitudes About Money

Read the following passage carefully. Then fill in each blank with a different word from the box. (Context clues will help you figure out which word goes in which blank.)

burden	**economical**	**extravagant**
security	**sympathize**	

Stacy and Ken have completely different attitudes about money. She is (1)___*economical*___ to the extreme, always <u>investigating</u> how to get the best deal on even the smallest purchase. Ken, on the other hand, is as (2)___*extravagant*___ as they come. He loves to spend money on anything that catches his eye. If there's a dime in his pocket, he feels that it's a (3)___*burden*___. He'll find something to spend it on just to be rid of it. Knowing she has money in the bank gives Stacy a feeling of (4)___*security*___, but Ken doesn't worry about the future.

Neither one can (5)___*sympathize*___ with the other's feelings. Each is <u>bewildered</u> by the other's "strange" behavior. Stacy sees Ken as wasteful and irresponsible, and Ken calls Stacy cheap. No one was surprised when those two got divorced.

SCORES:	Check 2 _____ %		Check 3 _____ %		Final Check _____ %

Enter your scores above and in the vocabulary performance chart on the inside back cover of the book.

4

Previewing the Words

Find out how many of the five words in this chapter you already know. Try to complete each sentence with the most suitable word from the list below. Use each word once.

Leave a sentence blank rather than guessing at an answer. Your purpose here is just to get a sense of the five words and what you may know about them.

determine	**dispose**	**evident**
preserve	**restore**	

1. Cody's concern for his sister was _____*evident*_____. He kept asking how she was feeling.

2. The twins are so alike that even their aunts and uncles can't always _____*determine*_____ which is which.

3. We need to _____*dispose*_____ of the junk in the garage. Let's put it on the curb for the garbage pickup.

4. Some people coat their unfinished wood houses with used motor oil in order to _____*preserve*_____ the wood against damage from moisture.

5. My brother plans to _____*restore*_____ his 1957 Chevrolet to its original condition. To do so, he'll need to replace several parts.

Now check your answers by turning to page 145. Fix any mistakes and fill in any blank spaces by writing in the correct answers. By doing so, you will complete this introduction to the five words.

You're now ready to strengthen your knowledge of the words you already know and to master the words you're only half sure of, or don't know at all. Turn to the next page.

Five Words in Context

Figure out the meanings of the following five words by looking *closely and carefully* at the sentences below. Doing so will prepare you for the matching test and practices that follow.

1 **determine**
(di'-tûr'-min)
-verb

  a. The doctor in the emergency room **determined** that Fred's ankle was sprained, not broken.

  b. I always take a calculator to the supermarket. Otherwise it takes too long to **determine** whether the "super-giant" size or the "family economy" size is the better buy.

2 **dispose**
(di-spōz')
-verb

  a. The sign said, "Lungs at work. Please **dispose** of all cigarettes, cigars, and pipes before entering."

  b. After losing forty pounds, Herb **disposed** of all the clothes that reminded him of his former size.

3 **evident**
(ev'-i-dənt)
-adjective

  a. The fact that my aunt dyes her hair is **evident**—her gray roots are easily seen.

  b. To make it **evident** that she didn't want to see James again, Crystal sent him back all his letters and gifts.

4 **preserve**
(pri-zûrv')
-verb

  a. Steps are being taken to **preserve** the remaining giant redwood trees of California and Oregon.

  b. To **preserve** its valuable old fabrics, the museum keeps them away from bright lights and extreme temperatures.

5 **restore**
(ri'-stōr')
-verb

  a. During the 1980s, millions of people gave money to **restore** the Statue of Liberty. The torch and the 1,600 iron bands that hold the copper skin to the frame were replaced.

  b. Amazingly, there have been cases where a bump on the head has **restored** the sight of a blind person.

Matching Words and Definitions

Check your understanding of the five words by matching each word with its definition. The sentences above will help you decide on the meaning of each word.

_c_	1. **determine**	a. obvious; clear
_d_	2. **dispose**	b. to bring back to a normal or former condition; repair
_a_	3. **evident**	c. to find out exactly; figure out
_e_	4. **preserve**	d. to throw or give away; get rid of
_b_	5. **restore**	e. to keep safe; protect; to keep in good condition

➤Check 1

Complete each sentence below with the correct word from the box. Use each word once.

determine	dispose	evident
preserve	restore	

1. When we say that something is _____*evident*_____, we mean that it can be clearly seen or clearly understood.

2. A good way to _____*determine*_____ which twin is which is to look for the mole on Beth's forehead.

3. If something has been _____*restore*_____(e)d, that means it was once in bad shape and has been fixed up in some way.

4. If something has been _____*preserve*_____(e)d, that means it has been taken good care of and kept in good shape.

5. There are several ways to _____*dispose*_____ of things you no longer want: put them in the garbage, recycle them, or give or sell them to someone who can use them.

Now check your answers to these questions by turning to page 145. Going over the answers carefully will help you prepare for the next three practices, for which answers are not given.

➤Check 2

Complete each sentence below with the correct word from the box. Use each word once.

determine	dispose	evident
preserve	restore	

1. Dan was out of danger within a few days after his heart attack, but it took several months of rest and medicine to fully _____*restore*_____ his health.

2. To _____*determine*_____ how much wallpaper you need, measure the walls of the room and then subtract the sizes of the windows and doors.

3. The park service forbids hunting in several state forests in order to _____*preserve*_____ the birds and animals living there.

4. The marks on the outside of our window make it _____*evident*_____ that someone tried to break into the house.

5. The Hendersons _____*dispose*_____ of all their food leftovers in a bin in their backyard. When the food rots, it makes good fertilizer for their garden.

➤ Check 3

A. Circle the letter of the best answer to each of the first four questions.

1. To *determine* means   a. to protect   b. to find   ⓒ to find out

2. *Evident* means   ⓐ easily seen   b. in good shape   c. famous

3. To *preserve* your car is to   ⓐ take good care of it   b. fix it up   c. sell it

4. To *dispose* of your car is to   a. take good care of it   b. fix it up   ⓒ sell it

B.   5. *Restore* is made up of the prefix *re-*, meaning "again," and the root *store*, meaning "construct." This adds up to the meaning: "construct again." (When you restore something, it's as if you are building it again.) Think of two more words beginning with *re-* that include the meaning "again." Then write them in the following blanks.

     Answers will vary.   _____

➤ Final Check: Fixing Up Furniture

Read the following passage carefully. Then fill in each blank with a different word from the box. (Context clues will help you figure out which word goes in which blank.)

determine	dispose	evident
preserve	restore	

I feel proud when I can fix up furniture that other people have (1)_____*dispose*_____d of. Rather than be <u>extravagant</u> and buy new furniture, I can take an old chair thrown out by a relative or an ugly bureau I've found in a neighbor's trash pile and (2)_____*restore*_____ it to its original condition. I often find a beautiful piece of furniture hidden under many coats of paint or varnish. At first it is hard to (3)_____*determine*_____ how good or bad the piece underneath really is. I must carefully remove the old paint or varnish. If it becomes (4)_____*evident*_____ that the quality of the piece of furniture is good, I sand it until it is smooth. Then I stain it to bring out the wood's natural lines and colors. Finally, I apply new varnish to (5)_____*preserve*_____ the wood from damage by water or heat. Fixing other people's castoffs has been an <u>economical</u> way for me to get some beautiful furniture.

SCORES: Check 2 _____ %   Check 3 _____ %   Final Check _____ %

Enter your scores above and in the vocabulary performance chart on the inside back cover of the book.

Previewing the Words

Find out how many of the five words in this chapter you already know. Try to complete each sentence with the most suitable word from the list below. Use each word once.

Leave a sentence blank rather than guessing at an answer. Your purpose here is just to get a sense of the five words and what you may know about them.

anxious	**convince**	**inferior**
overwhelm	**thorough**	

1. The mountain of papers waiting on his desk after vacation

   _____*overwhelm*_____(e)d Todd.

2. I've done a very _____*thorough*_____ review of my notes, so I feel well prepared for the test.

3. The second half of the movie was _____*inferior*_____ to the first part, which was much more interesting.

4. Mike had become very _____*anxious*_____ because his daughter was late getting home and the roads were icy.

5. The former drug addict went around to schools trying to _____*convince*_____ students that drugs are dangerous.

Now check your answers by turning to page 145. Fix any mistakes and fill in any blank spaces by writing in the correct answers. By doing so, you will complete this introduction to the five words.

You're now ready to strengthen your knowledge of the words you already know and to master the words you're only half sure of, or don't know at all. Turn to the next page.

Five Words in Context

Figure out the meanings of the following five words by looking *closely and carefully* at the sentences below. Doing so will prepare you for the matching test and practices that follow.

1 **anxious**
(angk'-shəs)
-*adjective*

    a. Dean was **anxious** about his new job. He worried about doing well and about whether he'll like the work.

    b. You seemed **anxious** before the test, but you look more relaxed now.

2 **convince**
(kən-vins')
-*verb*

    a. The lawyer is sure she can **convince** the jury that her client is innocent.

    b. Stephanie tried to **convince** her roommate that she didn't steal her necklace, but her roommate still didn't believe her.

3 **inferior**
(ɪn-ter'-e-ər)
-*adjective*

    a. The cheap shoes I bought were so **inferior** that they fell apart after only a few weeks.

    b. Joan's basketball skills are **inferior** to those of the other team members, but the coach believes Joan will improve quickly.

4 **overwhelm**
(ō'-vər-welm')
-*verb*

    a. You will **overwhelm** the children if you give too many instructions at one time.

    b. A gang of teens **overwhelmed** the old man, holding him down while they took his money.

5 **thorough**
(thûr'-ō)
-*adjective*

    a. After a **thorough** search of every corner of my apartment, I finally found my glasses—in my pocket.

    b. Before signing up your children at a day-care center, do a **thorough** check of how kind and well-trained the staff are.

Matching Words and Definitions

Check your understanding of the five words by matching each word with its definition. The sentences above will help you decide on the meaning of each word.

_d_	1. **anxious**	a. poor in quality; lower in value or quality (to)
_c_	2. **convince**	b. complete; very carefully done
_a_	3. **inferior**	c. to persuade by argument or proof
_e_	4. **overwhelm**	d. worried; troubled; fearful about what might happen
_b_	5. **thorough**	e. to overpower mentally, emotionally, or physically

➤Check 1

Complete each sentence below with the correct word from the box. Use each word once.

anxious	convince	inferior
overwhelm	thorough	

1. A grade of C is _____*inferior*_____ to a B.

2. Too much confusing work would _____*overwhelm*_____ anyone.

3. It should take proof to _____*convince*_____ a jury that someone is guilty.

4. Something frightening or troubling makes people _____*anxious*_____.

5. It usually takes more time to do a(n) _____*thorough*_____ job than a sloppy one.

Now check your answers to these questions by turning to page 145. Going over the answers carefully will help you prepare for the next three practices, for which answers are not given.

➤Check 2

Complete each sentence below with the correct word from the box. Use each word once.

anxious	convince	inferior
overwhelm	thorough	

1. A(n) _____*inferior*_____ paint won't last as long as a good quality one.

2. The _____*anxious*_____ child didn't want to sit in the dentist's chair.

3. I hope to _____*convince*_____ the interviewer that I'm qualified for the job.

4. The few palace guards were quickly _____*overwhelm*_____(e)d by the crowd of angry citizens.

5. Larry usually gives his apartment only a light cleaning, but every spring and fall, he does

   a more _____*thorough*_____ job.

➤ *Check 3*

Circle the letter of the best answer to each question.

1. The opposite of *anxious* is   a. skilled   b. wild   (c.) calm

2. The opposite of *inferior* is   (a.) high in quality   b. too expensive   c. heavy

3. The opposite of *thorough* is   a. small   b. natural   (c.) careless

4. If you *convince* me, you influence my   a. looks   (b.) opinion   c. income

5. One can be *overwhelmed*   a. physically   b. mentally
    (c.) both physically and mentally

➤ *Final Check:* Fear of Public Speaking

Read the following passage carefully. Then fill in each blank with a different word from the box. (Context clues will help you figure out which word goes in which blank.)

anxious	**convince**	**inferior**
overwhelm	**thorough**	

I get (1)_____*anxious*_____ even thinking about getting in front of the whole class to give my history report. I don't know why I feel so uneasy. I've done a(n) (2)____*thorough*____ job of preparing my report—I don't think I've left anything important out. I guess I compare myself to others and worry about whether my work is (3)_____*inferior*_____ to theirs. I hope that my fears won't (4)____*overwhelm*____ me and prevent me from doing a good job. I'll have to (5)____*convince*____ myself that as long as I've made an earnest effort, my report will be okay.

SCORES:	Check 2 _____%	Check 3 _____%	Final Check _____%

Enter your scores above and in the vocabulary performance chart on the inside back cover of the book.

Previewing the Words

Find out how many of the five words in this chapter you already know. Try to complete each sentence with the most suitable word from the list below. Use each word once.

Leave a sentence blank rather than guessing at an answer. Your purpose here is just to get a sense of the five words and what you may know about them.

comprehend	**dramatic**	**frank**
illustrate	**impression**	

1. The Giants made a _____*dramatic*_____ comeback and won the game.

2. To be _____*frank*_____, Jeffrey, your singing could be greatly improved.

3. The coach _____*illustrate*_____(e)d the proper way to shoot a free throw, but he missed the basket.

4. The fans are confused. They can't _____*comprehend*_____ why Wilson has been dropped from the team.

5. Yolanda left us with the _____*impression*_____ that she would be quitting her job soon.

Now check your answers by turning to page 145. Fix any mistakes and fill in any blank spaces by writing in the correct answers. By doing so, you will complete this introduction to the five words.

You're now ready to strengthen your knowledge of the words you already know and to master the words you're only half sure of, or don't know at all. Turn to the next page.

Five Words in Context

Figure out the meanings of the following five words by looking *closely and carefully* at the sentences below. Doing so will prepare you for the matching test and practices that follow.

1 **comprehend**
(kom'-pri-hend')
-*verb*

    a. Although my Japanese friend knew English pretty well when she came to this country, she did not **comprehend** such slang terms as "cool" and "gross."

    b. I cannot **comprehend** how a computer works, but at least I understand how to use one for writing papers.

2 **dramatic**
(dra-mat'-ik)
-*adjective*

    a. Because of their **dramatic** size and thick shells, ostrich eggs take forty minutes to hard-boil.

    b. To hold our attention, our gym teacher used **dramatic** movements, such as waving her arms or jumping.

3 **frank**
(frangk)
-*adjective*

    a. Mrs. Robins told her doctor, "Please be **frank** with me. If you've determined what is wrong with me, please tell me the truth."

    b. "To be **frank**," my sister said to me, "your new hairdo looks like you stuck your finger into an electrical socket."

4 **illustrate**
(il'-ə-strāt')
-*verb*

    a. Reverend Johnson **illustrated** his point about forgiving by telling a story about one victim who learned to forgive his attacker.

    b. The second graders wrote stories and then **illustrated** them with colorful pictures.

5 **impression**
(im-presh'-ən)
-*noun*

    a. My first **impression** of Leroy was that he was loud and ill-mannered, but spending time with him convinced me that under all the noise was a warm, friendly person.

    b. I had the **impression** that Vicky was coming on the ski trip, but at the last minute I learned that she'd never really planned to come.

Matching Words and Definitions

Check your understanding of the five words by matching each word with its definition. The sentences above will help you decide on the meaning of each word.

    _d_   1. **comprehend**   a. to make clear, as with an example, demonstration, or picture

    _b_   2. **dramatic**   b. very impressive or noticeable

    _e_   3. **frank**   c. a belief, opinion, or thought—often based on little information

    _a_   4. **illustrate**   d. to completely understand

    _c_   5. **impression**   e. honest and open; sincere

➤ *Check 1*

Complete each sentence below with the correct word from the box. Use each word once.

comprehend	dramatic	frank
illustrate	impression	

1. A _____*dramatic*_____ outfit is unusual and will attract attention.

2. Your first _____*impression*_____ of people is the same thing as your first opinion of them.

3. If you say that you _____*comprehend*_____ a math problem, it means you understand it well.

4. A _____*frank*_____ person is likely to tell you just what he or she thinks of your new hairdo, instead of giving you false compliments.

5. A good way to make an idea more clear is to _____*illustrate*_____ it in some way. To do so, you might use an example or a picture.

Now check your answers to these questions by turning to page 145. Going over the answers carefully will help you prepare for the next three practices, for which answers are not given.

➤ *Check 2*

Complete each sentence below with the correct word from the box. Use each word once.

comprehend	dramatic	frank
illustrate	impression	

1. Certain male baboons have _____*dramatic*_____ coloring—their faces and rumps have blue and scarlet markings.

2. If you read your psychology text before class, you will _____*comprehend*_____ the teacher's lecture better.

3. My _____*impression*_____ of Ved's father is that he is too busy with work and spends too little time with his family.

4. When Rosa gave a copy of her story to a friend to read, she said, "I don't want compliments. I want you to be _____*frank*_____ about what's good and bad in this."

5. The lecturer said that identical twins are born with similar personalities. To _____*illustrate*_____, he used the example of twins who had been separated at birth, but were still very much alike.

➤ *Check 3*

Circle the letter of the best answer to each question.

1. The opposite of *comprehend* is   a. realize   b. misunderstand   c. stop

2. The opposite of *frank* is   a. forgetful   b. dishonest   c. short

3. A *dramatic* hat would be   a. hard to see   b. common   c. unusual

4. A teacher might *illustrate* a lecture with   a. a drawing   b. a microphone   c. a quiz

5. Your *impression* of a teacher is what you   a. think of her   b. hope she'll be like
   c. forgot about her

➤ *Final Check:* Mrs. Thornton's Condition

Read the following passage carefully. Then fill in each blank with a different word from the box. (Context clues will help you figure out which word goes in which blank.)

comprehend	dramatic	frank
illustrate	impression	

Adults should be honest with children. I can (1)_____*illustrate*_____ this point by telling how I and my fellow first-graders suffered when our teacher had a baby. It wasn't that we didn't like babies or that we didn't like Mrs. Thornton. Most of us loved them both. The problem was that we didn't realize she was pregnant, so her (2) _____*dramatic*_____ growth frightened us. Could that happen to us some day? Would we balloon up for no reason? Also, we were worried about her. But even when we made our concern <u>evident</u> by asking what was happening to her, she gave us only silly answers like "I guess I ate too much breakfast!"

Finally, one day she didn't appear at school. Instead, our principal simply announced, "Mrs. Thornton will not be your teacher any more this year." We were left with the (3)_____*impression*_____ that something awful had happened to her. Maybe she had even burst. Fear and sadness <u>overwhelmed</u> us. Fortunately, the substitute teacher who took Mrs. Thornton's place saw our tearful faces and realized we did not (4)_____*comprehend*_____ the situation. She explained that Mrs. Thornton had just had a baby and that she was fine and very happy. But we could have been saved a lot of worry if the adults in our lives had just been more (5)_____*frank*_____ with us.

SCORES: Check 2 _____ %   Check 3 _____ %   Final Check _____ %

Enter your scores above and in the vocabulary performance chart on the inside back cover of the book.

UNIT ONE: *Test 1*

PART A
Complete each sentence with a word from the box. Use each word once.

appropriate	burden	communicate	deceive	determine
dispose	illustrate	inferior	security	theory

1. Letters are still a good way to _____*communicate*_____ to friends and family.

2. To _____*illustrate*_____ how much smell affects taste, our teacher had us eat a banana while smelling an onion.

3. My mother accidentally _____*dispose*_____(e)d of my bike—she sold it during her garage sale.

4. To increase her feeling of _____*security*_____ when she walks home from the bus at night, Elise learned karate.

5. When the children began screaming and throwing things on the bus, the driver yelled, "This is not _____*appropriate*_____ behavior!"

6. You can _____*determine*_____ how much your dog weighs by first weighing yourself and then weighing yourself again as you hold the dog.

7. Artie kept his wife from knowing he had lost his job. He _____*deceive*_____(e)d her by leaving the house each morning as if he were going to work.

8. Having our grandfather live with us was not a(n) _____*burden*_____. Not only was he easy to live with, he was very helpful around the house.

9. Emily went through life feeling _____*inferior*_____ to her brother, whom she believed was more intelligent and talented than she could ever be.

10. The police have a(n) _____*theory*_____ on who poured Tide in the town pool and why, but until they have more facts, they won't be able to charge anyone.

(Continues on next page)

PART B
Circle **C** if the italicized word is used **correctly.** Circle **I** if the word is used **incorrectly.**

C ⓘ 11. Fay is so *extravagant* that she purposely finds fault with waiters so that she can refuse to leave them a tip.

Ⓒ I 12. The teacher didn't want to *overwhelm* his new students, so he gave them just a little homework at first.

Ⓒ I 13. My 88-year-old grandmother says she *preserves* her good health by drinking ginger tea every day.

C ⓘ 14. It was perfectly *evident* that Joe could not read. Even his children didn't know.

Ⓒ I 15. Because I missed the first ten minutes of the movie, I didn't really *comprehend* the rest of the story.

Ⓒ I 16. Toby hardly saw the driver of the car that hit her, but her *impression* was that he was a blond teenager.

C ⓘ 17. My brother was so *earnest* when he agreed to mow the lawn that he hid our mower in a neighbor's garage.

C ⓘ 18. Rain had splashed across the note taped onto my front door. The words were thus so *legible* that I had no idea what the message was.

Ⓒ I 19. I used to be *anxious* about going to the dentist, but then I started going to Dr. Crane. He's so funny and nice that I just can't feel afraid of him.

C ⓘ 20. When vodka spilled on our coffee table, the alcohol completely *restored* a section of the table's shiny finish, right down to the bare wood.

Ⓒ I 21. Not trusting his sister's new boyfriend, Alf *investigated* the man's background and discovered that he had been married and divorced five times.

C ⓘ 22. Mac did a *thorough* job of cleaning our windows. They now looked like it was Halloween and they had been waxed by neighborhood children.

Ⓒ I 23. Since my sister skipped classes and assignments, it's hard for me to *sympathize* with her disappointment over failing algebra.

C ⓘ 24. I was *frank* enough to tell Edna she looked lovely in her new purple dress—even though it made her look like an oddly shaped eggplant.

Ⓒ I 25. English police are still *bewildered* by the 1934 murder of a woman whose body parts were found in two wooden trunks. Not only is the crime unsolved; the name of the victim is still unknown.

> **SCORE:** (Number correct) _____ x 4 = _____ %

Enter your score above and in the vocabulary performance chart on the inside back cover of the book.

UNIT ONE: Test 2

PART A: Synonyms
In the space provided, write the letter of the choice that is most nearly the **same** in meaning as the boldfaced word.

_a_	1. **a fiction**	**a)** falsehood	**b)** fact	**c)** books	**d)** words
_d_	2. **a theory**	**a)** research	**b)** thought	**c)** question	**d)** explanation
_b_	3. **to overwhelm**	**a)** climb	**b)** overpower	**c)** finish	**d)** rebuild
_c_	4. **security**	**a)** courage	**b)** danger	**c)** protection	**d)** happiness
_b_	5. **to determine**	**a)** go around	**b)** find out	**c)** delay	**d)** work
_c_	6. **an emotion**	**a)** movement	**b)** reason	**c)** feeling	**d)** goal
_a_	7. **an impression**	**a)** opinion	**b)** result	**c)** income	**d)** example
_a_	8. **to investigate**	**a)** examine	**b)** hire	**c)** accuse	**d)** admire
_d_	9. **to convince**	**a)** find guilty	**b)** annoy	**c)** join	**d)** persuade
_a_	10. **to preserve**	**a)** protect	**b)** serve	**c)** get ready	**d)** destroy
_c_	11. **dramatic**	**a)** noisy	**b)** hidden	**c)** very noticeable	
		d) very famous			
_b_	12. **economical**	**a)** funny	**b)** thrifty	**c)** wasteful	**d)** simple
_d_	13. **a burden**	**a)** sound	**b)** package	**c)** detail	**d)** hardship

(Continues on next page)

PART B: Antonyms
In the space provided, write the letter of the choice that is most nearly the **opposite** in meaning to the boldfaced word.

_d_ 14. **thorough**   **a)** blocked   **b)** gentle   **c)** famous   **d)** careless

_b_ 15. **to bewilder**   **a)** confuse   **b)** make clear to   **c)** curse   **d)** bless

_c_ 16. **legible**   **a)** not logical   **b)** slow   **c)** unclear   **d)** brief

_a_ 17. **to comprehend** **a)** misunderstand   **b)** go alone   **c)** be alike
                          d) fail

_a_ 18. **frank**   **a)** dishonest   **b)** unknown   **c)** not reliable
                          d) unfriendly

_b_ 19. **earnest**   **a)** likable   **b)** insincere   **c)** unable to earn
                          d) messy

_a_ 20. **to dispose of** **a)** keep   **b)** throw away   **c)** lose   **d)** find

_b_ 21. **to restore**   **a)** remember   **b)** destroy   **c)** shop   **d)** awaken

_b_ 22. **evident**   **a)** rare   **b)** hidden   **c)** wrong   **d)** everywhere

_c_ 23. **extravagant**   **a)** indoors   **b)** spending too much   **c)** thrifty
                          d) friendly

_d_ 24. **inferior**   **a)** outer   **b)** courageous   **c)** possible   **d)** better

_b_ 25. **to deceive**   **a)** build   **b)** tell the truth to   **c)** cheat   **d)** go up

---

SCORE: (Number correct) _____ x 4 = _____ %

Enter your score above and in the vocabulary performance chart on the inside back cover of the book.

Unit Two

Previewing the Words

Find out how many of the five words in this chapter you already know. Try to complete each sentence with the most suitable word from the list below. Use each word once.

Leave a sentence blank rather than guessing at an answer. Your purpose here is just to get a sense of the five words and what you may know about them.

conflict	stress	unanimous
vary	vicinity	

1. After the _____*stress*_____ of standing on her feet at work all week, Tina enjoys relaxing with a massage.

2. A certain lizard's colors _____*vary*_____ from brown to green, depending on what background it is sitting on.

3. The heavyweight champion kept his title with a _____*unanimous*_____ decision— all the referees agreed.

4. The United Nations urged the two countries to settle their

   _____*conflict*_____ over the borders.

5. Many children in our _____*vicinity*_____ get together for a Halloween party rather than going trick-or-treating.

Now check your answers by turning to page 145. Fix any mistakes and fill in any blank spaces by writing in the correct answers. By doing so, you will complete this introduction to the five words.

You're now ready to strengthen your knowledge of the words you already know and to master the words you're only half sure of, or don't know at all. Turn to the next page.

Five Words in Context

Figure out the meanings of the following five words by looking *closely and carefully* at the sentences below. Doing so will prepare you for the matching test and practices that follow.

1 **conflict**
(kən-flikt')
-noun

    a. When the **conflict** between the two diners became noisy, the restaurant manager asked them to settle their quarrel outside.

    b. Marsha's children often have **conflicts** about whose turn it is to <u>dispose</u> of the trash.

2 **stress**
(stres)
-noun

    a. My doctor said my headaches were caused by **stress**. He suggested that I think of ways to reduce the tension in my life.

    b. Phil and Angie are under a lot of **stress**. Angie's mother is very sick, Phil just lost his job, and they just learned that Angie is going to have twins.

3 **unanimous**
(yōō-nan'-ə-məs)
-adjective

    a. The voters were **unanimous** in electing me the president of the PTA. In fact, there was no other candidate to vote for.

    b. The jury's decision was **unanimous**. Every juror believed that the woman on trial had robbed the beauty parlor after getting a haircut.

4 **vary**
(vâr'-ē)
-verb

    a. There are often <u>dramatic</u> changes in weather along the coast. In one day, the temperature can **vary** by as much as 40 degrees.

    b. Matt never **varies** his lunch at work. Every day he eats a peanut butter and celery sandwich, pretzels, and a banana.

5 **vicinity**
(vi-sin'-i-tē)
-noun

    a. In the **vicinity** of the elementary school, the speed limit is fifteen miles an hour.

    b. The Johnsons decided not to purchase a house they liked when they learned that a nuclear power plant was in the **vicinity**.

Matching Words and Definitions

Check your understanding of the five words by matching each word with its definition. The sentences above will help you decide on the meaning of each word.

_d_	1. **conflict**	a. mental, physical, or emotional tension; strain
_a_	2. **stress**	b. to be different from one instance to another; to change
_e_	3. **unanimous**	c. the area near or around a place; neighborhood
_b_	4. **vary**	d. a quarrel or fight; a disagreement
_c_	5. **vicinity**	e. in full agreement

➤ *Check 1*

Complete each sentence below with the correct word from the box. Use each word once.

conflict	stress	unanimous
vary	vicinity	

1. If there's no disagreement among jurors, we say that the jury is _____*unanimous*_____.

2. Another way of saying you put variety in your diet is: you _____*vary*_____ your diet.

3. Anything that puts pressure on our <u>emotions</u>, bodies, or minds can be called _____*stress*_____.

4. Whether two people or groups are fighting with words or weapons, we can say they are having a _____*conflict*_____.

5. If someone lives in the _____*vicinity*_____ of your home, you would call that person a neighbor.

Now check your answers to these questions by turning to page 145. Going over the answers carefully will help you prepare for the next three practices, for which answers are not given.

➤ *Check 2*

Complete each sentence below with the correct word from the box. Use each word once.

conflict	stress	unanimous
vary	vicinity	

1. Two professions with a lot of _____*stress*_____ are police work and surgery. Both are careers with the tensions of life-and-death decisions.

2. Gerry is so afraid of _____*conflict*_____ with others that he always lets the other person have his own way.

3. After their collie died of old age, the Turner children were _____*unanimous*_____ in wanting to get another collie.

4. I get bored jogging on the same streets every day. In order to <u>restore</u> my interest, I've decided to _____*vary*_____ my route—each week I'll jog a different way.

5. The _____*vicinity*_____ of the school is a "Drug Free School Zone." People selling or carrying drugs in that area will receive the largest fines and the longest jail terms.

➤ *Check 3*

Circle **C** if the italicized word is used **correctly**, Circle **I** if the word is used **incorrectly**.

Ⓒ I   1. The main *conflict* between the union and the company was over salaries.

C Ⓘ   2. Unfortunately, the place where I work is in the *vicinity* of my home, about an hour and a half ride away.

C Ⓘ   3. The three friends were *unanimous* in their choice of movie. Two wanted to see a comedy, and one voted for a mystery.

Ⓒ I   4. As I study, I find that I get less tired if I *vary* my position from time by time, by changing chairs or just getting up and stretching.

C Ⓘ   5. I love going to the beach because the *stress* there is so great. I can just relax in the sun without a thought of work or school.

➤ *Final Check:* Traveling with Children

Read the following passage carefully. Then fill in each blank with a different word from the box. (Context clues will help you figure out which word goes in which blank.)

conflict	stress	unanimous
vary	vicinity	

Whether I'm driving in the (1)_____*vicinity*_____ of home or farther away, the trip seems to last longer if my kids are in the car. The minute we're on the road, the baby begins to cry and the older children start a major (2)_____*conflict*_____. These fights (3)_____*vary*_____ from time to time, but they usually have something to do with one of four main themes:

   1. One kid is in the front seat when it's another kid's turn.

   2. Someone who had a window seat last time got one again.

   3. One of the gang hates the music that another has turned on. (No single radio station has won the (4)_____*unanimous*_____ approval of the children.)

   4. One child feels another "is looking at me funny."

Now that I think about it, maybe I can <u>preserve</u> the peace and lower the level of (5)_____*stress*_____ in my life by sending the kids by bus and meeting them wherever we're going.

SCORES:	Check 2 _____ %	Check 3 _____ %	Final Check _____ %

Enter your scores above and in the vocabulary performance chart on the inside back cover of the book.

Previewing the Words

Find out how many of the five words in this chapter you already know. Try to complete each sentence with the most suitable word from the list below. Use each word once.

Leave a sentence blank rather than guessing at an answer. Your purpose here is just to get a sense of the five words and what you may know about them.

possess	**procedure**	**renew**
resource	**sufficient**	

1. We need to _____*renew*_____ our efforts to save oil.

2. Two weeks should be _____*sufficient*_____ time to complete your research papers.

3. The Dorseys _____*possess*_____ the oldest house in our community—it's almost a hundred years old.

4. In her will, our neighbor left to a nephew in California all her financial _____*resource*_____s—money, stocks, and bonds.

5. Firefighters must learn the _____*procedure*_____s for putting out different types of fires, including methods for handling grease and chemical fires.

Now check your answers by turning to page 145. Fix any mistakes and fill in any blank spaces by writing in the correct answers. By doing so, you will complete this introduction to the five words.

You're now ready to strengthen your knowledge of the words you already know and to master the words you're only half sure of, or don't know at all. Turn to the next page.

Five Words in Context

Figure out the meanings of the following five words by looking *closely and carefully* at the sentences below. Doing so will prepare you for the matching test and practices that follow.

1 **possess**
(pə-zes')
-*verb*

   a. I can't <u>comprehend</u> the desire to **possess** very expensive cars and jewelry. If I had more money, I'd spend it on travel.

   b. People who spend time in the <u>vicinity</u> of young children ought to **possess** plenty of patience.

2 **procedure**
(prə-sē'-jər)
-*noun*

   a. What **procedure** should I follow to become a citizen?

   b. Even kindergarten students can learn the **procedure** for reporting an emergency: Dial 911, give your name and address, and describe the problem.

3 **renew**
(ri-nōō')
-*verb*

   a. After helping to pay for their children's education, many parents barely have time to **renew** their savings in time for retirement.

   b. Elizabeth woke up feeling a little low, but a walk in the beautiful fall weather **renewed** her usual good spirits.

4 **resource**
(rē'-sōrs)
-*noun*

   a. West Virginia's natural **resources** include coal and timber.

   b. My children have more educational **resources**, such as films and computer programs, than I had when I went to school.

5 **sufficient**
(sə-fish'-ənt)
adjective

   a. The farmers were thankful that there was **sufficient** rain to save their crops.

   b. Brian's father told him, "When you bring the car home, make sure it has **sufficient** gas to get me to work tomorrow."

Matching Words and Definitions

Check your understanding of the five words by matching each word with its definition. The sentences above will help you decide on the meaning of each word.

   _e_ 1. **possess**   a. a method; the way in which something is done

   _a_ 2. **procedure**   b. as much as is needed; enough

   _d_ 3. **renew**   c. a source of support or help

   _c_ 4. **resource**   d. to make new or as if new again; restore

   _b_ 5. **sufficient**   e. to own; to have

➤ *Check 1*

Complete each sentence below with the correct word from the box. Use each word once.

possess	procedure	renew
resource	sufficient	

1. If you are always patient, we can say that you _____*possess*_____ lots of patience.

2. A country's _____*resource*_____s include all of its natural wealth—oil, gold, and so on.

3. A _____*procedure*_____ usually involves a series of steps.

4. If you say you have _____*sufficient*_____ time for an assignment, that means you have enough time to do it in.

5. A person could decide to _____*renew*_____ a magazine subscription or an old friendship.

Now check your answers to these questions by turning to page 145. Going over the answers carefully will help you prepare for the next three practices, for which answers are not given.

➤ *Check 2*

Complete each sentence below with the correct word from the box. Use each word once.

possess	procedure	renew
resource	sufficient	

1. Since I'd always believed Alvin was <u>frank</u> with me, it was difficult to _____*renew*_____ my trust in him after learning how he had lied to me.

2. The famous author writes in longhand. In fact, she doesn't even _____*possess*_____ a computer.

3. Victoria was nominated for class president, but she said she didn't have _____*sufficient*_____ self-confidence for the position.

4. I plan to save my money so that some day I'll have the financial _____*resource*_____s to open my own used clothing store for children.

5. Before we got to the fair, our father gave us a <u>thorough</u> explanation of the _____*procedure*_____ he wanted us to follow. We could go our separate ways, but in exactly two hours, we were to meet by the merry-go-round ticket booth.

➤ *Check 3*

Circle the letter of the best answer to each question.

1. A person might *possess*   a. clouds   (b.) musical talent   c. traffic

2. All *resources* are expected to be   a. new   b. bright   (c.) useful

3. A family with *sufficient* income   (a.) can live decently   b. is too poor
   c. has no income

4. A *procedure* can be   (a.) a process   b. a goal   c. a supply

5. To *renew* a forest, you must   a. chop   b. sell   (c.) plant

➤ *Final Check:* Saving Earth's Natural Supplies

Read the following passage carefully. Then fill in each blank with a different word from the box. (Context clues will help you figure out which word goes in which blank.)

possess	procedure	renew
resource	sufficient	

Once some of Earth's valuable (1)_____*resource*_____s are used up, it will be impossible to (2)_____*renew*_____ them. To <u>illustrate,</u> coal will someday be used up and gone forever.

We do, however, (3)_____*possess*_____ other important supplies that can be used over and over. Paper, metals, plastics and glass can be turned into new products again and again by means of recycling. It's up to each of us to have (4)_____*sufficient*_____ interest to learn about the recycling methods in our communities and then to follow those (5)_____*procedure*_____s.

SCORES:	Check 2 _____ %	Check 3 _____ %	Final Check _____ %

Enter your scores above and in the vocabulary performance chart on the inside back cover of the book.

Previewing the Words

Find out how many of the five words in this chapter you already know. Try to complete each sentence with the most suitable word from the list below. Use each word once.

Leave a sentence blank rather than guessing at an answer. Your purpose here is just to get a sense of the five words and what you may know about them.

current	**maintain**	**minimum**
originate	**reliable**	

1. Rita <u>varies</u> her wardrobe in order to keep up with _____*current*_____ fashion styles, but her sister wears the same basic styles, year after year.

2. The growth of suburban shopping malls has made it difficult for many downtown merchants to _____*maintain*_____ their businesses.

3. The sign on the Super Looper read, "The _____*minimum*_____ height required for riding this roller coaster is 52 inches."

4. I thought Leo would be a(n) _____*reliable*_____ worker, but he showed up late on Tuesday and not at all on Wednesday.

5. Mother's Day _____*originate*_____(e)d in 1908 when Anna Jarvis asked her church's Sunday School to set aside the anniversary of her mother's death to honor all mothers.

Now check your answers by turning to page 145. Fix any mistakes and fill in any blank spaces by writing in the correct answers. By doing so, you will complete this introduction to the five words.

You're now ready to strengthen your knowledge of the words you already know and to master the words you're only half sure of, or don't know at all. Turn to the next page.

Five Words in Context

Figure out the meanings of the following five words by looking *closely and carefully* at the sentences below. Doing so will prepare you for the matching test and practices that follow.

1 **current**
(kûr'-ənt)
-*adjective*

    a. In the past, many teachers hit students who misbehaved. Most **current** educators, however, consider violence wrong.

    b. Doctors once recommended total bed rest after surgery. However, **current** practice is to have patients walk as soon after an operation as possible.

2 **maintain**
(mān-tān')
-*verb*

    a. When driving, it's important to **maintain** a safe distance between your car and the car ahead of you.

    b. My brother must possess excellent study skills. He was able to **maintain** a B average throughout college while holding a full-time job.

3 **minimum**
(min'-ə-məm)
-*adjective*

    a. The **minimum** number of people allowed for each bus tour is eight. If fewer people sign up, the trip will be canceled.

    b. What's the **minimum** price you'll take for your car? I can't afford to pay much.

4 **originate**
(ə-rij'-ə-nāt')
-*verb*

    a. The ice-cream cone **originated** at the 1904 World's Fair in St. Louis. An ice-cream seller ran out of cups, so he wrapped a waffle around the ice cream and sold it that way.

    b. Baseball didn't really **originate** in Cooperstown, New York, in 1839. It must have started earlier, as the sport was mentioned as early as 1744 in English publications.

5 **reliable**
(ri-lī'-ə-bəl)
-*adjective*

    a. Joe Sherman is a **reliable** mechanic. You can count on him to fix whatever is wrong with your car at a reasonable price.

    b. It's important to me to have a **reliable** babysitter. It would make me very anxious to leave my baby with someone I couldn't trust to do a careful job.

Matching Words and Definitions

Check your understanding of the five words by matching each word with its definition. The sentences above will help you decide on the meaning of each word.

_d_	1. **current**	a. smallest allowed or possible; least; lowest
_c_	2. **maintain**	b. dependable; trustworthy
_a_	3. **minimum**	c. to continue; carry on; keep in existence
_e_	4. **originate**	d. modern; existing now; in general use or practice today
_b_	5. **reliable**	e. to come into being; begin

➤ *Check 1*

Complete each sentence below with the correct word from the box. Use each word once.

current	maintain	minimum
originate	reliable	

1. We can say that the place where a river starts is where it _____*originate*_____s.
2. A worker who is honest and does his job carefully would be called a
   _____*reliable*_____ worker.
3. We might refer to styles that are widely worn today as _____*current*_____ fashions.
4. The opposite of the highest salary the company allows would be its
   _____*minimum*_____ salary.
5. You must keep up a B average to keep your football uniform. In other words, if you
   don't _____*maintain*_____ good grades, you're off the team.

Now check your answers to these questions by turning to page 145. Going over the answers carefully will help you prepare for the next three practices, for which answers are not given.

➤ *Check 2*

Complete each sentence below with the correct word from the box. Use each word once.

current	maintain	minimum
originate	reliable	

1. The reporter said his story is from a _____*reliable*_____ source, someone who can be depended on to tell the truth.
2. To get the _____*minimum*_____ number of trick-or-treaters on Halloween nights, simply pass out prunes instead of candy.
3. When I was a child, a loaf of bread cost about thirty-five cents. _____*Current*_____ prices go as high as around two dollars a loaf.
4. If you want to _____*maintain*_____ good health throughout your life, get in the habit of eating a healthy diet and getting <u>sufficient</u> exercise.
5. The custom of a man opening the door for a woman _____*originate*_____(e)d when women wore large skirts with hoops that made it hard for them to reach the doorknob.

➤ *Check 3*

A. Circle the letter of the best answer to each question.

1. To learn about *current* events, read   a. a history book   (b.) the newspaper   c. the comics

2. To *maintain* a garden,   a. avoid it   (b.) plant and weed all season
                                          c. photograph it

3. The *minimum* number of people in a moving car should be
                                          (a.) one   b. five   c. six.

4. The umbrella *originated* when it was   a. open   (b.) invented   c. wet

B.   5. *Reliable* is made up of the word *rely* and the suffix *-able*. Those two parts of the word add up to its meaning: "able to be relied upon." Think of two more words that end in *-able* and write them in the blanks below.

     _____*Answers will vary.*_____   _____

➤ *Final Check:* Toasters

Read the following passage carefully. Then fill in each blank with a different word from the box. (Context clues will help you figure out which word goes in which blank.)

current	**maintain**	**minimum**
originate	**reliable**	

     Although the practice of eating toasted bread (1)_____*originate*_____(e)d about 4600 years ago, the pop-up electric toaster was not invented until 1919. These early pop-up toasters were not very (2)_____*reliable*_____—they broke down often. Also, they weren't able to (3)_____*maintain*_____ an even temperature, but grew hotter and hotter with each piece of bread toasted. Some very <u>inferior</u> machines even popped the toast all the way across the room. Over the years, toasters have certainly improved. (4)_____*Current*_____ ones give us (5)_____*minimum*_____ problems with repairs and temperature control.

SCORES:	Check 2 _____ %	Check 3 _____ %	Final Check _____ %

Enter your scores above and in the vocabulary performance chart on the inside back cover of the book.

Previewing the Words

Find out how many of the five words in this chapter you already know. Try to complete each sentence with the most suitable word from the list below. Use each word once.

Leave a sentence blank rather than guessing at an answer. Your purpose here is just to get a sense of the five words and what you may know about them.

advise	**deprive**	**hesitate**
objection	**penalize**	

1. Woody Allen says he has no _____*objection*_____ to dying. He just doesn't want to be there when it happens.

2. Although it was raining out, the elderly man did not _____*hesitate*_____ to help the woman who had fallen.

3. The park ranger said, "I _____*advise*_____ you to hang your food from a tree if you don't want the bears to get it."

4. I don't think Sharon would mind much if her parents stopped her allowance, but if they _____*deprive*_____(e)d her of her soap operas, she'd be really upset.

5. Since no student confessed to putting egg salad on the fan, the teacher _____*penalize*_____(e)d the entire class, keeping them after school for as long as it took to clean up the room.

Now check your answers by turning to page 145. Fix any mistakes and fill in any blank spaces by writing in the correct answers. By doing so, you will complete this introduction to the five words.

You're now ready to strengthen your knowledge of the words you already know and to master the words you're only half sure of, or don't know at all. Turn to the next page.

Five Words in Context

Figure out the meanings of the following five words by looking *closely and carefully* at the sentences below. Doing so will prepare you for the matching test and practices that follow.

1 **advise**
(ad-vīz')
-verb

   a. I'd like to **advise** Alan to break up with Elaine, but I know he'll get angry if I make that suggestion.

   b. When I hurt my back, my doctor **advised** me to stay in bed for at least a week. I agreed, even though a week without pay was a real financial <u>burden</u>.

2 **deprive**
(di-prīv')
-verb

   a. Isaac's parents **deprived** him of his allowance because he hadn't done his household jobs all week.

   b. Dad complains that his low-fat, low-calorie diet **deprives** him of everything he enjoys eating

3 **hesitate**
(hez'-i-tāt')
-verb

   a. On certain game shows, if a player **hesitates** before giving an answer, another player might answer first.

   b. At first Jack **hesitated** to let Julie know that he liked her, but he finally got up enough nerve to tell her.

4 **objection**
(əb-jek'-shən)
-noun

   a. My only **objection** to eating corn on the cob is the unattractive way it sticks on one's teeth.

   b. Granddad had a strong **objection** to boys wearing long hair. Once when my father refused to get a haircut, Granddad cut one side of his hair when he was asleep.

5 **penalize**
(pē'-nə-līz')
-verb

   a. Whenever my parents heard I had been punished at school, they **penalized** me again at home.

   b. "The next time you're so late," my girlfriend said, "I'll **penalize** you by whipping your tongue with a hot pepper."

Matching Words and Definitions

Check your understanding of the five words by matching each word with its definition. Look above at the sentences in "Five Words in Context" as needed to decide on the meaning of each word.

_e_	1. **advise**	a. to take away from; to keep from having or enjoying
_a_	2. **deprive**	b. to be slow to speak, act, or decide
_b_	3. **hesitate**	c. a reason for being against; a dislike
_c_	4. **objection**	d. to punish
_d_	5. **penalize**	e. to give advice to; suggest

➤Check 1

Complete each sentence below with the correct word from the box. Use each word once.

advise	deprive	hesitate
objection	penalize	

1. It used to be more common for teachers to _____*penalize*_____ students by hitting them.

2. My aunt is not a <u>reliable</u> patient; she rarely does what her doctor _____*advise*_____s her to do.

3. Prison _____*deprive*_____s people of much of their freedom.

4. I _____*hesitate*_____d to answer the teacher's question because I wasn't certain if he had called on me or the student behind me.

5. My _____*objection*_____ to that comedian is that his jokes often hurt other people.

Now check your answers to these questions by turning to page 145. Going over the answers carefully will help you prepare for the next three practices, for which answers are not given.

➤Check 2

Complete each sentence below with the correct word from the box. Use each word once.

advise	deprive	hesitate
objection	penalize	

1. The judge _____*penalize*_____d the young thief with 100 hours of volunteer work.

2. Since losing my job, I've had to _____*deprive*_____ myself of costly recreation, such as going to the movies or eating at expensive restaurants.

3. When my friend told me about all the <u>conflicts</u> she and her husband were having, I _____*advise*_____d her to see a counselor.

4. Dale had a strong _____*objection*_____ to the wallpaper her husband picked out for their living room. "It looks like a doctor's waiting room," she complained.

5. "I want your meal to be very special," the waiter told the couple celebrating their 40th wedding anniversary. "Don't _____*hesitate*_____ to ask me for anything."

➤Check 3

Circle the letter of the best answer to each question.

1. You would *advise* a friend by   a. smiling   (b.) giving your opinion   c. leaving
2. When you *hesitate,* you   (a.) wait   b. take   c. punish
3. People have an *objection* to   a. money   (b.) crime   c. weather
4. The **opposite** of *deprive* is   a. wish   b. clean   (c.) give
5. The **opposite** of *penalize* is   a. avoid   b. surprise   (c.) reward

➤*Final Check:* A Mean Man

Read the following passage carefully. Then fill in each blank with a word from the box. (Context clues will help you figure out which word goes in which blank.) Use each word once.

advise	**deprive**	**hesitate**
objection	**penalize**	

Mr. Barker says that he has no (1)_____*objection*_____ to kids—as long as they don't come into his yard, as long as they don't (2)_____*deprive*_____ him of peace and quiet, and as long as they don't grow up to be teenagers.

Neighborhood kids say he's the meanest man they ever met. Who can blame them? If he sees them choosing up sides for a ballgame in the street, for example, he doesn't (3)_____*hesitate*_____ a minute. He runs right to his window and yells, "You can't do that in front of MY house!" The kids are afraid of him, but they yell back that the street belongs to everybody. "Well, I (4)_____*advise*_____ you to watch your step!" he responds. "If you break my window or step on my flowers, you will be (5)_____*penalize*_____d." Then he slams his window shut—until the next time he sees a chance to be mean. Maybe a hard life has made Mr. Barker the way he is, but it's hard to <u>sympathize</u> with someone like him.

SCORES:	Check 2 _____ %	Check 3 _____ %	**Final Check** _____ %

Enter your scores above and in the vocabulary performance chart on the inside back cover of the book.

11

Previewing the Words

Find out how many of the five words in this chapter you already know. Try to complete each sentence with the most suitable word from the list below. Use each word once.

Leave a sentence blank rather than guessing at an answer. Your purpose here is just to get a sense of the five words and what you may know about them.

conscious	external	incredible
internal	remedy	

1. Much of the outside of an artichoke is too tough to eat, but the

   _____*internal*_____ part is tender and delicious.

2. The sight of all the birds on the field was _____*incredible*_____. It looked as if the whole field had turned black.

3. Your cheery telephone call was just the _____*remedy*_____ for Sandy's loneliness.

4. The social studies teacher's only objection to her students was that they didn't

   seem at all _____*conscious*_____ of anything going on in the world outside of their small town.

5. The Rands got rid of any _____*external*_____ sign that they were home—they parked their car around the corner, turned off all the lights facing the street, and left their newspaper in the driveway.

Now check your answers by turning to page 146. Fix any mistakes and fill in any blank spaces by writing in the correct answers. By doing so, you will complete this introduction to the five words.

You're now ready to strengthen your knowledge of the words you already know and to master the words you're only half sure of, or don't know at all. Turn to the next page.

Five Words in Context

Figure out the meanings of the following five words by looking *closely and carefully* at the sentences below. Doing so will prepare you for the matching test and practices that follow.

1 **conscious**
(kon'-shəs)
-adjective

   a. About an hour after his heart operation, the patient became **conscious** enough to smile at his wife.

   b. As Arlene gave her speech to the class, she was **conscious** of people whispering in the back of the room.

2 **external**
(ik-stûr'-nəl)
-adjective

   a. The **external** appearances of the two houses were similar, but the homes differed quite a bit on the inside.

   b. When my grandmother first came to America, she was given her very first orange. As no one <u>advised</u> her to remove its **external** layer, she began to eat the peeling.

3 **incredible**
(in-kred'-ə-bəl)
-adjective

   a. It's **incredible** that a cat could survive 43 days locked in a crate, <u>deprived</u> of food and water, and yet it has happened.

   b. A good film can make an **incredible** story (like the one about E.T.) seem believable while you watch it.

4 **internal**
(in-tûr'-nəl)
-adjective

   a. Animals such as the lobster and crab do not have **internal** skeletons like most animals. Instead, their bodies are supported by a hard outer shell.

   b. The car looks terrific, so you'd never guess that some of its **internal** parts—the motor, brakes, and heater—need major repair.

5 **remedy**
(rem'-i-dē)
-noun

   a. Aunt Harriet's **remedy** for a cold was to wear garlic around her neck. I'm sure it never cured her cold, but at least nobody came close enough to her to catch it.

   b. There's no quick **remedy** for a broken heart, but time will eventually bring some healing.

Matching Words and Definitions

Check your understanding of the five words by matching each word with its definition. Look above at the sentences in "Five Words in Context" as needed to decide on the meaning of each word.

  d   1. **conscious**   a. so unusual as to seem impossible; unbelievable

  e   2. **external**   b. inner; inside

  a   3. **incredible**   c. cure; relief

  b   4. **internal**   d. awake; aware of

  c   5. **remedy**   e. outer; outside

➤ *Check 1*

Complete each sentence below with the correct word from the box. Use each word once.

conscious	external	incredible
internal	remedy	

1. Do you think there will ever be a _____*remedy*_____ for the common cold?

2. The _____*external*_____ part of an orange is its peel.

3. The _____*internal*_____ part of an orange is its sweet, juicy flesh.

4. The Grand Canyon is the most _____*incredible*_____ sight I've ever seen. It's so huge, it's hard to believe even when you're standing there looking at it.

5. Two meanings of "_____*conscious*_____" are "being awake" and "noticing something."

Now check your answers to these questions by turning to page 146. Going over the answers carefully will help you prepare for the next three practices, for which answers are not given.

➤ *Check 2*

Complete each sentence below with the correct word from the box. Use each word once.

conscious	external	incredible
internal	remedy	

1. Norman Cousins felt that laughter is a powerful _____*remedy*_____ for any illness.

2. The moon landing of 1969 was a(n) _____*incredible*_____ achievement.

3. I peel vegetables grown with pesticides because much of the chemicals remain in their _____*external*_____ layer.

4. Gene didn't appear too badly injured by the car accident, but doctors soon discovered he had serious _____*internal*_____ injuries.

5. I wasn't _____*conscious*_____ of putting my keys in the refrigerator, but I guess I did it because there they are, right beside the Swiss cheese.

➤Check 3

Circle **C** if the italicized word is used **correctly.** Circle **I** if the word is used **incorrectly.**

C ⓘ 1. While I was *conscious,* I dreamt I was drowning. Suddenly, I awoke and discovered it was pouring outside.

Ⓒ I 2. In 1858, one slave made an *incredible* escape from Virginia—he hid in a box that was being shipped to Philadelphia.

C ⓘ 3. A *remedy* for some adults' anger is the mental or physical abuse of their children.

Ⓒ I 4. I had no *external* signs of injury after the car accident.

Ⓒ I 5. But I did suffer from *internal* injuries that included a bruised liver and lungs.

➤ Final Check: Coming Out of a Coma

Read the following passage carefully. Then fill in each blank with a word from the box. (Context clues will help you figure out which word goes in which blank.)

conscious	external	incredible
internal	remedy	

"Hi, Mom," Francis said.

To his mother, these were the best words she had ever heard. Her son was (1)_____*conscious*_____ again, after ten weeks in a coma following an accident.

The idea that Francis was again aware of his surroundings was (2)_____*incredible*_____. He had been gone from this world for so long that it seemed he'd never return. Whenever Ms. King had visited her son at the hospital, he had been completely still. There were no (3)_____*external*_____ signs that he was thinking or feeling anything. He was, as the doctors put it, "a vegetable." But Ms. King maintained the hope that he still had some (4)_____*internal*_____ life. Could he, perhaps, hear her words? Could he feel her hand squeezing his? She tried to reach him in any way she could during her daily visits.

Now, although Ms. King knew there was no quick (5)_____*remedy*_____ for her son's serious injuries, the simple words "Hi, Mom" gave her hope that he could, someday, live a full life again.

SCORES:	Check 2 _____ %	Check 3 _____ %	Final Check _____ %

Enter your scores above and in the vocabulary performance chart on the inside back cover of the book.

Previewing the Words

Find out how many of the five words in this chapter you already know. Try to complete each sentence with the most suitable word from the list below. Use each word once.

Leave a sentence blank rather than guessing at an answer. Your purpose here is just to get a sense of the five words and what you may know about them.

assume	**exhaust**	**maximum**
objective	**protest**	

1. It was so hot on the Fourth of July that the ice supply at our party was
   _____*exhaust*_____(e)d before noon.

2. Paul was found guilty and <u>penalized</u> for the robbery. He was sentenced to a
   _____*maximum*_____ of seven years in jail, but got out after only four years.

3. My sister's _____*objective*_____ is to be a fashion designer.

4. Hundreds of parents _____*protest*_____(e)d the closing of their local grade
   school, so the mayor decided to try to raise money to keep it open.

5. Although I usually _____*assume*_____ people are telling the truth, I take it
   for granted that much of what Karen says is false. She thinks nothing of <u>deceiving</u>
   even her best friends.

Now check your answers by turning to page 146. Fix any mistakes and fill in any blank spaces by writing in the correct answers. By doing so, you will complete this introduction to the five words.

You're now ready to strengthen your knowledge of the words you already know and to master the words you're only half sure of, or don't know at all. Turn to the next page.

Five Words in Context

Figure out the meanings of the following five words by looking *closely and carefully* at the sentences below. Doing so will prepare you for the matching test and practices that follow.

1 **assume**
(ə-sōōm')
-*verb*

   a. The Clarks **assumed** that the motel they were staying in had a coffee shop, so they were surprised to learn they'd have to drive somewhere else to eat.

   b. We can't **assume** the sun will shine during an outdoor wedding. When it comes to weather, one mustn't take anything for granted.

2 **exhaust**
(ig-zôst')
-*verb*

   a. Frieda has such a sweet nature that even teaching twenty-six children all day doesn't **exhaust** her patience.

   b. Chopping firewood all afternoon **exhausted** Ken. Afterward, he collapsed on the sofa and fell asleep.

3 **maximum**
(mak'-sə-məm)
-*adjective*

   a. The sign in the elevator told the **maximum** weight it could safely carry.

   b. Three hundred miles per hour is the **maximum** speed for this airplane; it can go no faster.

4 **objective**
(əb-jek'-tiv)
-*noun*

   a. The **objective** of the workshop on time management is to teach people to get the most done in the <u>minimum</u> amount of time.

   b. Chris and Tomas thought about starting a business together, but they soon realized their **objectives** were different. Chris wanted to make a lot of money, while Tomas wanted to help people in the community.

5 **protest**
(prə-test')
-*verb*

   a. The animal rights organization **protested** the misuse of animals in medical experiments.

   b. "Stop it," Billy's mother **protested.** "You can't pour blue food coloring in the mashed potatoes."

Matching Words and Definitions

Check your understanding of the five words by matching each word with its definition. Look above at the sentences in "Five Words in Context" as needed to decide on the meaning of each word.

_d_	1. **assume**	a. to speak strongly against; to express disapproval
_e_	2. **exhaust**	b. greatest possible; highest
_b_	3. **maximum**	c. a purpose; goal
_c_	4. **objective**	d. to suppose to be true; take for granted
_a_	5. **protest**	e. to use up; to tire greatly

➤ *Check 1*

Complete each sentence below with the correct word from the box. Use each word once.

assume	exhaust	maximum
objective	protest	

1. Whatever you work toward is called your _____*objective*_____.
2. The opposite of the lowest speed allowed on a highway is the _____*maximum*_____ speed.
3. If you don't like a company's policy, why not _____*protest*_____ it by writing a strong letter of complaint?
4. Rather than _____*assume*_____ it would not rain on our outdoor wedding, we rented a large tent, just in case.
5. Two meanings of "_____*exhaust*_____" are "to use something up" and "to tire someone greatly."

Now check your answers to these questions by turning to page 146. Going over the answers carefully will help you prepare for the next three practices, for which answers are not given.

➤ *Check 2*

Complete each sentence below with the correct word from the box. Use each word once.

assume	exhaust	maximum
objective	protest	

1. We were glad the long car trip did not _____*exhaust*_____ Bethany.
2. Six is the _____*maximum*_____ number of books that you can check out from our library at one time.
3. Doug, a carpenter, never _____*assume*_____s that he and a customer agree on a project until a contract is signed.
4. My _____*objective*_____ in visiting public gardens was to get some ideas for plantings around my own house.
5. If you didn't want the hair stylist to cut your hair so short, why didn't you _____*protest*_____ when he started?

➤*Check 3*

A. Circle **C** if the italicized word is used **correctly**. Circle **I** if the word is used **incorrectly**.

C Ⓘ 1. Whenever Lee gets angry, he throws whatever *objectives* he can lay his hands on.

C Ⓘ 2. The *maximum* temperature in Minnesota all year was 35 degrees below zero.

Ⓒ I 3. Unless you call to say you're staying at work, I'll *assume* you'll be home for dinner.

C Ⓘ 4. I was too shy to ask Glen on a date face to face, so I decided to *protest* in a singing telegram.

B. 5. In *exhaust,* the prefix *ex-* means "out." (Exhaust can be defined as "to empty out.") Stressing this meaning of *ex-*, write a definition for one of the following words:

exit, exhale, expel: _____*To go out (leave) / To breathe out / To force out*_____

➤*Final Check:* **The Office Doughnut Contest**

Read the following passage carefully. Then fill in each blank with a different word from the box. (Context clues will help you figure out which word goes in which blank.)

assume	**exhaust**	**maximum**
objective	**protest**	

"Are you telling me there are no doughnuts left? I don't believe it!" Joan said. "How could a huge supply of doughnuts be (1)_____*exhaust*_____(e)d already?"

"I don't know how," Fran answered. "I just know none are left."

"When I brought three dozen doughnuts in this morning, I (2)_____*assume*_____(e)d I'd get to eat at least one," Joan said. "After all, the (3)_____*maximum*_____ number of people who ever work in this place is ten. Today, Sue isn't even here. It's <u>incredible</u> that the other eight of you could eat thirty-six doughnuts in less than three hours."

Then Fran and Joan became aware that, in the office next door, three grown men were tossing doughnuts across the room. Their (4)_____*objective*_____ was to throw the doughnuts onto the pencils held up by three other grown men.

"I don't believe you guys!" Joan (5)_____*protest*_____(e)d. "Just you wait. Next time it's my turn to bring in the doughnuts, I'll bring in cream- and jelly-filled doughnuts, and we'll see how you play your little game then."

SCORES:	**Check 2** ____ %		**Check 3** ____ %		**Final Check** ____ %

Enter your scores above and in the vocabulary performance chart on the inside back cover of the book.

UNIT TWO: *Test 1*

PART A
Complete each sentence with a word from the box. Use each word once.

incredible	maintain	maximum	penalize	procedure
protest	stress	unanimous	vary	vicinity

1. As _____*incredible*_____ as it seems, the Nile River in Africa has frozen over at least twice.

2. When we lived in the _____*vicinity*_____ of a train, we got so used to the noise that we stopped hearing it.

3. Marie's moods _____*vary*_____ with the weather. She's cheerful when the sun shines and gloomy when it's cloudy out.

4. In court, the decision of the jury must be _____*unanimous*_____. If even one juror has a different opinion, the decision doesn't count.

5. I try to _____*maintain*_____ my friendship with Sarah, but it's difficult to keep a relationship going when we're separated by so many miles.

6. It doesn't seem fair that the _____*maximum*_____ age for workers in our company is 65. Even the president has to retire at the early age of 66.

7. Dr. Hoffman said that some new _____*procedure*_____s for treating cancer are quicker and more successful than the old methods.

8. The chickens _____*protest*_____ loudly whenever anyone steals their eggs out from under them.

9. My parents used to _____*penalize*_____ me for misbehaving at the supper table by making me sit on the stairs, where I could hear the conversation but not take part in it.

10. Even good events can create _____*stress*_____ in people's lives. For example, researchers have found there's even more strain in getting married than in being fired from one's job.

(Continues on next page)

PART B
Circle **C** if the italicized word is used **correctly.** Circle **I** if the word is used **incorrectly.**

C Ⓘ 11. My only *objective* to Mimi is that spending time with her is more boring than reruns of the weather report.

Ⓒ I 12. Spaghetti-like noodles did not *originate* in Italy, as is commonly thought, but in China.

C Ⓘ 13. The *minimum* possible grade in our school is an A. No teacher ever gives an A+.

Ⓒ I 14. Just because Donald is quiet, don't *assume* that he's stupid.

C Ⓘ 15. The house's *internal* appearance is neat, but inside, it's a mess.

C Ⓘ 16. My long lunch hour *deprives* me of the time to take a short walk after lunch.

Ⓒ I 17. One natural *resource* that we don't have to worry about losing for a while is sunshine.

C Ⓘ 18. A nap *exhausted* me enough so that I could stay up and work on my paper till midnight.

Ⓒ I 19. As she read in the living room, Anna became *conscious* of loud voices in her parents' room.

C Ⓘ 20. After using the *external* part of onions and potatoes in a meal, I use their peels in making a broth.

Ⓒ I 21. My parents *advised* me not to charge anything that I can't pay for in full at the end of the month.

C Ⓘ 22. The union members' main *objection* to the contract was that the medical benefits were excellent.

Ⓒ I 23. Even though the police believe Frank robbed the liquor store, they don't yet have *sufficient* evidence to arrest him.

Ⓒ I 24. The *current* belief about dinosaurs is that they were not stupid, as was once thought, but intelligent creatures that took good care of their young.

C Ⓘ 25. I was always interested in art until I took an art course in high school. The teacher *renewed* my interest in drawing and painting by constantly finding fault with my work.

SCORE: (Number correct) _____ x4 = _____ %

Enter your score above and in the vocabulary performance chart on the inside back cover of the book.

UNIT TWO: Test 2

PART A: Synonyms
In the space provided, write the letter of the choice that is most nearly the **same** in meaning as the boldfaced word.

_a_ 1. **unanimous**   **a)** in full agreement   **b)** not together   **c)** unhappy
    d) pleased

_c_ 2. **to possess**   **a)** be lawful   **b)** lose   **c)** have   **d)** disobey

_b_ 3. **to exhaust**   **a)** leave   **b)** use up   **c)** put out   **d)** do

_a_ 4. **a procedure**   **a)** method   **b)** protection   **c)** example   **d)** reward

_d_ 5. **to assume**   **a)** collect   **b)** deny   **c)** attend   **d)** suppose

_c_ 6. **reliable**   **a)** well-known   **b)** related   **c)** trustworthy
    d) trusting

_b_ 7. **the stress**   **a)** location   **b)** tension   **c)** rule   **d)** time

_d_ 8. **to deprive of**   **a)** suggest to   **b)** believe   **c)** disapprove of
    d) take away from

_b_ 9. **the vicinity**   **a)** sight   **b)** neighborhood   **c)** energy   **d)** possibility

_c_ 10. **an objection to**   **a)** goal   **b)** thing   **c)** reason against   **d)** reason

_a_ 11. **a resource**   **a)** supply   **b)** reason   **c)** goal   **d)** method

_c_ 12. **to hesitate**   **a)** wonder   **b)** cause   **c)** delay   **d)** break

_b_ 13. **an objective**   **a)** reason against   **b)** purpose   **c)** puzzle   **d)** supply

(Continues on next page)

PART B: Antonyms
In the space provided, write the letter of the choice that is most nearly the **opposite** in meaning to the boldfaced word.

_a_ 14. **a conflict**   a) agreement   b) argument   c) gift   d) idea

_a_ 15. **to originate**   a) end   b) begin   c) remember   d) forget

_b_ 16. **external**   a) outer   b) inner   c) upper   d) lower

_c_ 17. **to penalize**   a) admire   b) free   c) reward   d) entertain

_a_ 18. **to vary**   a) keep the same   b) warn   c) change   d) attack

_d_ 19. **a remedy**   a) need   b) cure   c) extra   d) poison

_c_ 20. **sufficient**   a) comfortable   b) organized   c) not enough
d) unimportant

_d_ 21. **current**   a) electrical   b) by hand   c) not attractive
d) out-of-date

_b_ 22. **incredible**   a) amazing   b) believable   c) not natural   d) asleep

_a_ 23. **to maintain**   a) stop   b) believe   c) doubt   d) ignore

_c_ 24. **maximum**   a) biggest   b) most   c) least   d) hardest

_d_ 25. **to protest**   a) broadcast   b) hide   c) notice   d) approve of

SCORE: (Number correct) _____ x 4 = _____ %

Enter your score above and in the vocabulary performance chart on the inside back cover of the book.

Unit Three

Previewing the Words

Find out how many of the five words in this chapter you already know. Try to complete each sentence with the most suitable word from the list below. Use each word once.

Leave a sentence blank rather than guessing at an answer. Your purpose here is just to get a sense of the five words and what you may know about them.

accompany	desperate	pursue
rejection	scarce	

1. The reason for the army's _____*rejection*_____ of Paul was that he had many allergies.

2. My father went back to school to _____*pursue*_____ a degree in computer science.

3. I don't want to go to the concert alone. Will you _____*accompany*_____ me there?

4. Many types of cancer aren't as _____*desperate*_____ as they used to be. With proper treatment, many victims overcome their illness.

5. In mid-summer, when there are plenty of strawberries, their price is reasonable, but in the winter when they are _____*scarce*_____, the price is very high.

Now check your answers by turning to page 146. Fix any mistakes and fill in any blank spaces by writing in the correct answers. By doing so, you will complete this introduction to the five words.

You're now ready to strengthen your knowledge of the words you already know and to master the words you're only half sure of, or don't know at all. Turn to the next page.

Five Words in Context

Figure out the meanings of the following five words by looking *closely and carefully* at the sentences below. Doing so will prepare you for the matching test and practices that follow.

1 **accompany**
(ə-kum'-pə-nē)
-verb

   a. The Myers asked my sister to **accompany** them to the seashore, to help take care of their young children.

   b. In popular music, words usually **accompany** the tune. In much classical music, there are no words to go with the notes.

2 **desperate**
(des'-pər-it)
-adjective

   a. Our situation was **desperate**—our boat had a leak, our supplies were <u>exhausted</u>, and there was no help in sight.

   b. The earthquake victims are **desperate** for food and clothing.

3 **pursue**
(pər-soō')
-verb

   a. Two teens **pursued** the man who had grabbed Peggy's purse, but they couldn't catch him.

   b. Victor plans to **pursue** an acting career in New York City; his <u>objective</u> is to become a great actor, not a great star.

4 **rejection**
(ri-jek'-shən)
-noun

   a. My brother was upset when he received a letter of **rejection** from a college he wanted to attend.

   b. Nita wasn't too disturbed when she didn't get a part in the play she had tried out for. "If you can't handle **rejection,** you shouldn't be an actor," she said.

5 **scarce**
(skârs)
-adjective

   a. Since 1909 pennies are **scarce,** I <u>assume</u> the one I own is worth a lot of money.

   b. In the book *The Long Winter*, the author tells about the time food was so **scarce** that she and her family lived on little more than bread for weeks.

Matching Words and Definitions

Check your understanding of the five words by matching each word with its definition. Look above at the sentences in "Five Words in Context" as needed to decide on the meaning of each word.

_c_	1. **accompany**	a.	rare; hard to get; not enough to meet the demand
_d_	2. **desperate**	b.	a saying "no" (to a request or desire); refusal; denial
_e_	3. **pursue**	c.	to go along with; to be together with
_b_	4. **rejection**	d.	nearly hopeless; having a great need or desire
_a_	5. **scarce**	e.	to chase; to try to get or succeed in

➤Check 1

Complete each sentence below with the correct word from the box. Use each word once.

accompany	desperate	pursue
rejection	scarce	

1. The **opposite** of "acceptance" is "_____*rejection*_____."

2. The **opposite** of "plentiful" is "_____*scarce*_____."

3. Do you like ketchup to _____*accompany*_____ your french fries, or do you prefer them alone?

4. Two meanings of "_____*desperate*_____" are "without much chance for things to work out well" and "needing or wanting something badly."

5. Two meanings of "_____*pursue*_____" are "to follow (someone or something) in order to catch or pass" and "to aim for a goal."

Now check your answers to these questions by turning to page 146. Going over the answers carefully will help you prepare for the next three practices, for which answers are not given.

➤Check 2

Complete each sentence below with the correct word from the box. Use each word once.

accompany	desperate	pursue
rejection	scarce	

1. When my uncle was a boy, money and space were so _____*scarce*_____ that he had to share a bed with two of his brothers.

2. Don't let the fear of _____*rejection*_____ keep you from asking people out on dates. Everyone gets refused sooner or later.

3. State police _____*pursue*_____d the escaped killer until they caught him in the next county.

4. When a member of Alcoholics Anonymous is _____*desperate*_____ for a drink, he or she is supposed to call another AA member for help.

5. Maria was too proud to ask someone to _____*accompany*_____ her to the doctor's office, but I got the <u>impression</u> that she wanted me to go with her.

➤Check 3

Circle **C** if the italicized word is used **correctly**. Circle **I** if the word is used **incorrectly**.

C ⓘ 1. Ned sounded *desperate.* He must have won the state lottery.

Ⓒ I 2. In children's picture books, the pictures are often *accompanied* by very few words.

C ⓘ 3. Our weeds have become so *scarce* that they've taken over our lawn.

C ⓘ 4. My husband celebrated the *rejection* of my request for a raise by cooking and serving a fancy dinner.

Ⓒ I 5. The children love to *pursue* each other through their grandmother's huge old house, playing hide-and-seek in all the small, dark spaces.

➤*Final Check:* Barbara's Date with Her Cousin

Read the following passage carefully. Then fill in each blank with a different word from the box. (Context clues will help you figure out which word goes in which blank.)

accompany	desperate	pursue
rejection	scarce	

Barbara can finally laugh about the time twenty years ago when she was so (1)_____*desperate*_____ for a date that she paid her cousin $25 to go with her to the senior prom. She admits that dates were pretty (2)_____*scarce*_____ for her in high school. However, when the prom tickets first went on sale, Barbara hoped that some handsome fellow would fall for her charms and ask her to the prom, and maybe even to go steady. It didn't happen.

Back then, people didn't think it was very "ladylike" behavior to (3)_____*pursue*_____ a boy, but Barbara really wanted to go to the prom. Despite her fear of (4)_____*rejection*_____, she got up her nerve to ask Gary. He already had a date. So she asked Walt and then Chuck. They also said no.

One week before the prom, she called her cousin. He said, "Okay, but it will cost you." He said $5 was for being willing to (5)_____*accompany*_____ her and $15 was for not telling anyone at the prom that they were related.

SCORES: Check 2 _____ %	Check 3 _____ %	Final Check _____ %	

Enter your scores above and in the vocabulary performance chart on the inside back cover of the book.

Previewing the Words

Find out how many of the five words in this chapter you already know. Try to complete each sentence with the most suitable word from the list below. Use each word once.

Leave a sentence blank rather than guessing at an answer. Your purpose here is just to get a sense of the five words and what you may know about them.

appeal	**establish**	**potential**
variety	**wholesome**	

1. The blood bank _____*appeal*_____(e)d to people in the community to donate blood because supplies were scarce.

2. Bonny's teacher says she has the _____*potential*_____ to get A's and B's; she just has to study more.

3. When my father contacted me for the first time in ten years, I felt a

   _____*variety*_____ of <u>emotions</u>, including anger, excitement, and regret.

4. William Boyce _____*establish*_____(e)d the Boy Scouts of America in 1910 after an English Boy Scout helped him when he was lost in London on a foggy night.

5. Most parents would rather see their teenager doing some _____*wholesome*_____ activity, such as working or skating, instead of hanging around a street corner.

Now check your answers by turning to page 146. Fix any mistakes and fill in any blank spaces by writing in the correct answers. By doing so, you will complete this introduction to the five words.

You're now ready to strengthen your knowledge of the words you already know and to master the words you're only half sure of, or don't know at all. Turn to the next page.

Five Words in Context

Figure out the meanings of the following five words by looking *closely and carefully* at the sentences below. Doing so will prepare you for the matching test and practices that follow.

1 **appeal**
(ə-pēl')
-verb

   a. Every year, Jerry Lewis goes on TV to **appeal** to viewers for money to help people with muscular dystrophy.

   b. No matter how I look at it, celery and carrots just don't **appeal** to me as much as a hot fudge sundae does.

2 **establish**
(e-stab'-lish)
-verb

   a. The first lending library was **established** in Scotland in 1725.

   b. When adult children move back in with their parents, everyone should sit down together and **establish** some house rules they all agree on.

3 **potential**
(pə ten'-shəl)
-noun

   a. The new video store's excellent location adds to its **potential** for success.

   b. Everyone agrees that Carlos has the **potential** of being a major league baseball player. To become that good, he must continue to work hard.

4 **variety**
(və-rī'-i-tē)
-noun

   a. In the spring, the woods contain a **variety** of wildflowers, including bluebells, crocus, and violets.

   b. Instead of being a **variety** of colors, all of Gale's clothes were lavender or purple.

5 **wholesome**
(hōl'-səm)
-adjective

   a. Ken used to spend hours in a smoky video arcade where drug dealers hung out, but now he prefers more **wholesome** activities, like sports and music.

   b. We now know smoking is not **wholesome,** but early cigarette ads claimed physical and mental benefits for smokers.

Matching Words and Definitions

Check your understanding of the five words by matching each word with its definition. Look above at the sentences in "Five Words in Context" as needed to decide on the meaning of each word.

d	1. **appeal**	a. to bring into being; to set up
a	2. **establish**	b. tending to improve the character, the mind, or the body
e	3. **potential**	c. a number of different kinds; assortment
c	4. **variety**	d. to make an important request (often *to* someone *for* something); to attract
b	5. **wholesome**	e. possibility; an underlying ability that may or may not develop

➤*Check 1*

Complete each sentence below with the correct word from the box. Use each word once.

appeal	establish	potential
variety	wholesome	

1. An acorn has the _____*potential*_____ of being an oak tree.

2. Every family must _____*establish*_____ its own rules.

3. Starting every day with exercise is more _____*wholesome*_____ than starting every day with a cigarette.

4. Clint has worked in a _____*variety*_____ of positions, including trucker, carpenter, and rancher.

5. Two meanings of "_____*appeal*_____" are "to ask for something" and "to be of interest."

Now check your answers to these questions by turning to page 146. Going over the answers carefully will help you prepare for the next three practices, for which answers are not given.

➤*Check 2*

Complete each sentence below with the correct word from the box. Use each word once.

appeal	establish	potential
variety	wholesome	

1. Loretta plans to _____*establish*_____ her new T-shirt business near Chicago.

2. Because of a terrible disease, my cousin's bones have the _____*potential*_____ to break with even the smallest bump or fall.

3. My family enjoys a _____*variety*_____ of activities at the lake, including swimming, boating and fishing.

4. Grandfather wanted me to work in the family business, but since I'm a vegetarian, being a butcher certainly doesn't _____*appeal*_____ to me.

5. Boys Town provided a _____*wholesome*_____ way of life for boys, many of whom had been <u>desperate</u> because they had no home or person to care for them.

➤Check 3

Circle the letter of the best answer to each question.

1. An outfit that *appeals* is   ⓐ attractive   b. too small   c. expensive
2. The opposite of *establish* is   a. write   b. interest   ⓒ end
3. A person's *potential*   a. will develop   ⓑ may develop   c. cannot develop
4. There is often *variety* in a box of   a. raisins   ⓑ fancy candies   c. popcorn
5. The opposite of *wholesome* is   a. trusting   b. helpful   ⓒ harmful

➤*Final Check:* **Big Brothers and Sisters**

Read the following passage carefully. Then fill in each blank with a different word from the box. (Context clues will help you figure out which word goes in which blank.)

appeal	**establish**	**potential**
variety	**wholesome**	

   This week, the local Big Brother/Big Sister Agency (1)_____*appeal*_____(e)d to the community for volunteers. The organization is looking for men and women who are willing to (2)_____*establish*_____ a new friendship with a young boy or girl from a single-parent home.   The only requirement for becoming a volunteer is the desire to become friends with the children, to help them to stay in school, and to choose (3)_____*wholesome*_____ activities that will keep them out of trouble. Volunteers can do a(n) (4)_____*variety*_____ of things with their little "brothers" or "sisters," such as <u>accompanying</u> them to the park or going out to eat. Whatever activities they choose, volunteers will play an important part in the children's lives, assisting them to develop their (5)_____*potential*_____ to live rich lives and become good citizens.

SCORES: Check 2 _____ %   Check 3 _____ %   Final Check _____ %

Enter your scores above and in the vocabulary performance chart on the inside back cover of the book.

Previewing the Words

Find out how many of the five words in this chapter you already know. Try to complete each sentence with the most suitable word from the list below. Use each word once.

Leave a sentence blank rather than guessing at an answer. Your purpose here is just to get a sense of the five words and what you may know about them.

emphasis	**interpret**	**propose**
ultimate	**vague**	

1. Saying they learned a lot in class is the _____*ultimate*_____ compliment students can pay a teacher.

2. Different religions _____*interpret*_____ the Bible differently.

3. Brad's father put a lot of _____*emphasis*_____ on doing well in sports, but little attention to doing well in school.

4. On the phone, the encyclopedia salesman promised me a "really good deal," but when I asked for the exact cost, his answer was _____*vague*_____.

5. As the family thought over what to do on their free Saturday, their little boy _____*propose*_____(e)d a trip to the natural history museum to see the dinosaurs.

Now check your answers by turning to page 146. Fix any mistakes and fill in any blank spaces by writing in the correct answers. By doing so, you will complete this introduction to the five words.

You're now ready to strengthen your knowledge of the words you already know and to master the words you're only half sure of, or don't know at all. Turn to the next page.

Five Words in Context

Figure out the meanings of the following five words by looking *closely and carefully* at the sentences below. Doing so will prepare you for the matching test and practices that follow.

1 **emphasis**
(em'-fə-sis)
-noun

    a. Trudy didn't say much during her first two committee meetings. She felt the **emphasis** for a new member should be on listening and learning, not on talking.

    b. In my Spanish class, there was too much **emphasis** given to reading and not enough to speaking.

2 **interpret**
(in-tûr'-prit)
-verb

    a. After Ray had a dental x-ray made, the dentist sat down with him to **interpret** the results.

    b. How should I **interpret** the fact that, while we were friendly yesterday, Jean refused to speak to me today?

3 **propose**
(prə-pōz')
-verb

    a. Our little brother **proposed** buying our parents a puppy for Christmas, but instead we gave them a coffee grinder.

    b. Rafael was obviously too tired to study, so his mother **proposed** that he take a nap and get back to work later.

4 **ultimate**
(ul'-tə-mit)
-adjective

    a. Although her husband had affairs before, Suzanne felt his affair with her own sister was the **ultimate** stab in the back.

    b. Roger and Marilyn's **ultimate** goal is to run a restaurant offering dishes from a <u>variety</u> of countries.

5 **vague**
(vāg)
-adjective

    a. On the essay test, give specific answers, not **vague** ones.

    b. Ben had only a **vague** idea of what yeast was. He knew it was used to make beer and bread, but he wasn't sure what it did.

Matching Words and Definitions

Check your understanding of the five words by matching each word with its definition. Look above at the sentences in "Five Words in Context" as needed to decide on the meaning of each word.

_b_	1. **emphasis**	a. to suggest; offer for thinking over or accepting
_d_	2. **interpret**	b. special attention; importance given to something
_a_	3. **propose**	c. unclear; not expressed or understood in an exact way
_e_	4. **ultimate**	d. to explain the meaning of; make sense of
_c_	5. **vague**	e. greatest; highest possible

➤Check 1

Complete each sentence below with the correct word from the box. Use each word once.

emphasis	interpret	propose
ultimate	vague	

1. Your _____*ultimate*_____ goal is the one you hope to reach one day.

2. A clear answer is the opposite of a(n) _____*vague*_____ answer.

3. Your boss will put the most _____*emphasis*_____ on the project he considers most important.

4. Since I didn't understand the results of my blood test, the doctor _____*interpret*_____(e)d it for me.

5. We encourage our children to _____*propose*_____ weekend activities so we can consider their suggestions when planning.

Now check your answers to these questions by turning to page 146. Going over the answers carefully will help you prepare for the next three practices, for which answers are not given.

➤Check 2

Complete each sentence below with the correct word from the box. Use each word once.

emphasis	interpret	propose
ultimate	vague	

1. My little sister _____*interpret*_____(e)d the street sign "Slow—Children" to mean that the children nearby were slow.

2. Many schools give too much _____*emphasis*_____ to learning facts and not enough to learning to think.

3. Every year Emily _____*propose*_____s that we go ice-skating on New Year's Eve, and every year we do something else.

4. When I ask my children where they're going, I don't accept _____*vague*_____ answers. I want to know exactly where they'll be.

5. This year I'm visiting three states, and my _____*ultimate*_____ goal is to visit every state in the country.

➤ *Check 3*

Circle **C** if the italicized word is used **correctly.** Circle **I** if the word is used **incorrectly.**

C Ⓘ 1. In my English class, the *emphasis* is on reading, so we spend more time on writing than on reading.

Ⓒ I 2. I *interpreted* Hank's sudden friendliness to mean he needed another loan.

Ⓒ I 3. The *ultimate* reason for giving to charity is to help others, not to lower one's taxes.

C Ⓘ 4. The instructions were so *vague* that I found it easy to operate our new electric toenail clipper.

Ⓒ I 5. I rejected the price *proposed* by the used car dealer.

➤ *Final Check:* Differences in a Gym Program

Read the following passage carefully. Then fill in each blank with a word from the box. (Context clues will help you figure out which word goes in which blank.)

emphasis	interpret	propose
ultimate	vague	

Last spring, some parents spoke to the school board about the school gym program. The parents protested the difference in programs offered to boys and girls. The boys were taught many active sports and given good equipment. They had the chance to join several teams. For girls, however, the (1)_____ *emphasis* _____ in gym was on dancing and exercise. They had no teams and little equipment.

Why were there such big differences between the two programs? The school district's rules about physical education were (2)_____ *vague* _____. Since they didn't say exactly what should be taught, each school (3)_____ *interpret* _____(e)d the rules in its own way.

The parents (4)_____ *propose* _____(e)d allowing both boys and girls of the Walnut Street School to use all the gym equipment there. And they appealed for some sports teams to be organized for the girls. They pointed out that girls have as much potential and need for physical fitness as boys do. Their (5) _____ *ultimate* _____ goal was to give all the children an equal gym experience.

SCORES:	**Check 2** _____ %	**Check 3** _____ %	**Final Check** _____ %		

Enter your scores above and in the vocabulary performance chart on the inside back cover of the book.

16

Previewing the Words

Find out how many of the five words in this chapter you already know. Try to complete each sentence with the most suitable word from the list below. Use each word once.

Leave a sentence blank rather than guessing at an answer. Your purpose here is just to get a sense of the five words and what you may know about them.

challenge	**fertile**	**peculiar**
surplus	**transform**	

1. There's a story about King Midas, who ___*transform*___(e)d whatever he touched into gold.

2. Kendall realizes that becoming a marine is a big ___*challenge*___.

3. Our ___*surplus*___ wheat is sold to other countries.

4. Sophie and her sisters joke about being especially ___*fertile*___. Among the four of them, they have twenty-three children.

5. My brother thinks my chip and dip sandwiches are ___*peculiar*___, but I don't think they're as odd as the peanut butter and tuna sandwiches he eats.

Now check your answers by turning to page 146. Fix any mistakes and fill in any blank spaces by writing in the correct answers. By doing so, you will complete this introduction to the five words.

You're now ready to strengthen your knowledge of the words you already know and to master the words you're only half sure of, or don't know at all. Turn to the next page.

Five Words in Context

Figure out the meanings of the following five words by looking *closely and carefully* at the sentences below. Doing so will prepare you for the matching test and practices that follow.

1 **challenge**
(chal'-inj)
-noun

   a. Ginny enjoys rock climbing. It's a difficult **challenge**, but she feels very proud after making a climb.

   b. When the babysitter arrived, he stared at the four active little boys he was expected to watch. "This will be quite a **challenge**," he sighed.

2 **fertile**
(fûr'-tl)
-adjective

   a. Because of its **fertile** soil, Iowa has many farms.

   b. Our daughter's pet hamsters were so **fertile** that we ended up selling many baby hamsters back to the pet store.

3 **peculiar**
(pi-kyōōl'-yər)
-adjective

   a. Jack didn't know why people were giving him **peculiar** looks until he realized there was a hole in his pants.

   b. The female pigeon has a **peculiar** requirement for laying eggs—she must see another pigeon. If none is available, her own reflection in a mirror will do.

4 **surplus**
(sûr'-plus)
-adjective

   a. More and more restaurants are donating their **surplus** food to homeless people.

   b. The Barkleys had more kitchen supplies than they needed, so they gave their **surplus** dishes and pans to their son, who had just moved into his own apartment.

5 **transform**
(trans-fôrm')
-verb

   a. I plan to **transform** this messy attic into an attractive office.

   b. The magician seemed to **transform** a chicken egg into an egg the size of a basketball.

Matching Words and Definitions

Check your understanding of the five words by matching each word with its definition. Look above at the sentences in "Five Words in Context" as needed to decide on the meaning of each word.

  b   1. **challenge**   a. odd; strange

  d   2. **fertile**   b. anything that calls for a special effort

  a   3. **peculiar**   c. to change in form or appearance

  e   4. **surplus**   d. producing or able to produce much fruit, large crops, or many children

  c   5. **transform**   e. extra; more than what is used or needed

➤Check 1

Complete each sentence below with the correct word from the box. Use each word once.

challenge	**fertile**	**peculiar**
surplus	**transform**	

1. Babysitting with a lot of children isn't easy—it's a _____*challenge*_____.

2. If we say that you've _____*transform*_____ed a room, we mean you've changed it a lot.

3. It's better for a restaurant's _____*surplus*_____ food to feed homeless people than to be thrown away.

4. Another way to say that something is quite unusual is to call it "_____*peculiar*_____."

5. The word "_____*fertile*_____" can apply to anything fruitful—fruitful soil, plants, and animals.

Now check your answers to these questions by turning to page 146. Going over the answers carefully will help you prepare for the next three practices, for which answers are not given.

➤Check 2

Complete each sentence below with the correct word from the box. Use each word once.

challenge	**fertile**	**peculiar**
surplus	**transform**	

1. Just one can of spinach _____*transform*_____s Popeye from a weakling into a hero with large muscles.

2. Max and Helen had more clothes than they needed, so they donated their _____*surplus*_____ clothes to a thrift store.

3. I can't imagine what that _____*peculiar*_____ odor is from—it's like a mixture of burning tires and freshly cut grass.

4. For Will, it's always a welcome _____*challenge*_____ to try to get a date with a girl who isn't interested in him at first.

5. If land is always planted with the same crop, it will become less _____*fertile*_____. Changing crops from one year to the next keeps soil rich.

➤ Check 3

Circle the letter of the best answer to each question.

1. When taking on a *challenge,* you must (a.) try   b. rush   c. write

2. A *fertile* apple tree will grow   a. old   (b.) many apples   c. in all climates

3. A *peculiar* color for lipstick is   a. pink   (b.) blue   c. red

4. When you *transform* something, you   a. buy it   b. give it away   (c.) make it different

5. A *surplus* of workers may lead to   a. hiring   (b.) layoffs   c. greater profits

➤ Final Check: Don's Garden

Read the following passage carefully. Then fill in each blank with a different word from the box. (Context clues will help you figure out which word goes in which blank.)

challenge	fertile	peculiar
surplus	transform	

Don decided to (1)_____*transform*_____ his weed-filled yard into a vegetable garden. He hoped the soil was (2)_____*fertile*_____ enough to grow a rich supply of vegetables.

He didn't have to worry. Before long, he had the first six of many ripe squashes. (One was such a (3)_____*peculiar*_____ shape that it reminded him of a little toe with a big bunion.) Then came the tomatoes. There were no red ones for days—until the evening he found sixty-three, begging to be picked. The next day, there were twenty-seven more. Don used some of what he grew, but he had many (4)_____*surplus*_____ squash and tomatoes to give to neighbors and friends.

The squash and tomato crops made up for the fact that only a few peppers and carrots grew. All in all, Don found growing his own vegetables to be a worthwhile (5)_____*challenge*_____. It was also a good way to establish ties with his new neighbors—and to improve his backyard without a lawn mower.

SCORES:	Check 2 _____%	Check 3 _____%	Final Check _____%

Enter your scores above and in the vocabulary performance chart on the inside back cover of the book.

Previewing the Words

Find out how many of the five words in this chapter you already know. Try to complete each sentence with the most suitable word from the list below. Use each word once.

Leave a sentence blank rather than guessing at an answer. Your purpose here is just to get a sense of the five words and what you may know about them.

complicate	**conscience**	**counsel**
detect	**transparent**	

1. Marion's sudden interest in finance was a _____*transparent*_____ effort to get to know the new accountant at work.

2. My husband said he quit smoking, but I _____*detect*_____(e)d the smell of smoke in our basement last night.

3. The college president _____*counsel*_____(e)d students to get a well-rounded education, rather than limit themselves to one subject.

4. It used to be simpler to figure out one's taxes, but the new laws have greatly _____*complicate*_____(d) the procedure for filling out tax forms.

5. When Chet's mother asked if he'd broken the window, Chet said no, but she interpreted his refusal to look at her to mean he had a guilty _____*conscience*_____.

Now check your answers by turning to page 146. Fix any mistakes and fill in any blank spaces by writing in the correct answers. By doing so, you will complete this introduction to the five words.

You're now ready to strengthen your knowledge of the words you already know and to master the words you're only half sure of, or don't know at all. Turn to the next page.

Five Words in Context

Figure out the meanings of the following five words by looking *closely and carefully* at the sentences below. Doing so will prepare you for the matching test and practices that follow.

1 **complicate**
(kom'-plə-kāt')
-*verb*

   a. Cooking for a crowd is a <u>challenge</u>, so don't **complicate** matters with fancy dishes. Keep it simple.

   b. I wish I hadn't **complicated** my morning by agreeing to pick up both Faye and Rich on the way to the meeting. They live on opposite ends of the city.

2 **conscience**
(kon'-shəns)
-*noun*

   a. After Lena stole the compact disc, her **conscience** bothered her so much that she couldn't enjoy listening to the music.

   b. It's <u>peculiar</u> but true that some criminals don't have a **conscience**. They really don't believe it's wrong to cheat, steal, and kill.

3 **counsel**
(koun'-səl)
-*verb*

   a. After Lana's boyfriend slapped her, her sister **counseled** her to break up with him.

   b. My adviser at school **counseled** me to work fewer hours each week so that I'll have more time to study.

4 **detect**
(di-tekt')
-*verb*

   a. If you **detect** a gas leak in your house, leave immediately and call for help.

   b. Rachel did not say directly that she disliked Ron, but I **detected** a dislike in her tone of voice.

5 **transparent**
(trans-pâr'-ənt)
-*adjective*

   a. I thought the glass in the door was **transparent** until I got close. Then I realized it was a mirror—I was seeing myself, not someone on the other side.

   b. Burt's remark that he had liked my new dress was a **transparent** lie. He couldn't even remember what it looked like.

Matching Words and Definitions

Check your understanding of the five words by matching each word with its definition. Look above at the sentences in "Five Words in Context" as needed to decide on the meaning of each word.

  b   1. **complicate**   a. to give advice or guidance

  e   2. **conscience**   b. to make difficult; involve with many parts or details

  a   3. **counsel**   c. to discover; find out; notice

  c   4. **detect**   d. allowing light to pass through so that objects on the other side can be seen; easily recognized

  d   5. **transparent**   e. a sense of what is right or wrong in one's behavior

➤ *Check 1*

Complete each sentence below with the correct word from the box. Use each word once.

complicate	**conscience**	**counsel**
detect	**transparent**	

1. How many hours a week would you _____*counsel*_____ a student to work?
2. If you _____*complicate*_____ a job, you make it harder to do.
3. You can _____*detect*_____ much that is unsaid through the tone of a person's voice.
4. A cruel person doesn't have much of a _____*conscience*_____.
5. Two meanings of "_____*transparent*_____" are "easily seen through" and "easily recognized, or obvious."

Now check your answers to these questions by turning to page 146. Going over the answers carefully will help you prepare for the next three practices, for which answers are not given.

➤ *Check 2*

Complete each sentence below with the correct word from the box. Use each word once.

complicate	**conscience**	**counsel**
detect	**transparent**	

1. The magazine article _____*counsel*_____s people to take a ride in a used car before buying it.
2. My parents were ready to buy the house until they _____*detect*_____(e)d a huge crack in an external basement wall.
3. Our little get-together to watch the game was going to be simple until Ricki _____*complicate*_____(e)d matters by inviting a dozen neighbors over.
4. The windows in our building are _____*transparent*_____ only to people on the inside. We can see outside, but people outdoors cannot see inside.
5. Two-year-old Jason is beginning to have a _____*conscience*_____. He ran to hide behind the sofa after putting his whole set of blocks into the fish tank.

➤ Check 3

Circle the letter of the best answer to each question.

1. The **opposite** of *complicate* is make   a. difficult   b. less expensive   (c.) simpler
2. Our *conscience* is mainly based on our   a. taste   (b.) morals   c. skills
3. A person who *counsels* gives   (a.) suggestions   b. difficulties   c. admiration
4. You could *detect* a gas leak by   a. studying   (b.) smelling   c. planning
5. A *transparent* purpose is   a. weak   (b.) clear   c. unusual

➤ Final Check: Lizzie's Lies

Read the following passage carefully. Then fill in each blank with a word from the box. (Context clues will help you figure out which word goes in which blank.)

complicate	conscience	counsel
detect	transparent	

Lizzie was a good employee at the photography store, except for one serious fault. Rather than ever admit she was wrong, she would lie to cover up her mistakes. Her (1)____*conscience*____ often bothered her after she lied, but she would ignore it. One day, however, one of her lies was (2)____*detect*____(e)d in a way that embarrassed her terribly. A customer had dropped off two rolls of film to be developed. Lizzie put them in her pocket and forgot about them. When the customer returned the next day for the prints, Lizzie remembered the rolls in her pocket but insisted that someone else in the store must have lost them. As she pretended to help look for the "missing" film, she leaned over to check a low shelf. The hidden rolls fell from her pocket. The store grew quiet as Lizzie realized that the customer, her boss, and all her co-workers had seen through her (3)____*transparent*____ lie. She left the store in shame. Later that afternoon, however, she returned to ask her boss for his advice. She expected to be fired, but she wanted him to (4)____*counsel*____ her on how to apologize to the customer and how to stop telling lies. He kindly offered Lizzie another chance at work, but warned her that telling lies would only (5)____*complicate*____ her life instead of making it easier. Lizzie remembered that lesson whenever she was tempted to lie her way out of a sticky situation.

SCORES:	Check 2 _____ %	Check 3 _____ %	Final Check _____ %

Enter your scores above and in the vocabulary performance chart on the inside back cover of the book.

18

Previewing the Words

Find out how many of the five words in this chapter you already know. Try to complete each sentence with the most suitable word from the list below. Use each word once.

Leave a sentence blank rather than guessing at an answer. Your purpose here is just to get a sense of the five words and what you may know about them.

dependent	preference	principal
solitary	suitable	

1. A _____*solitary*_____ living rose was left on the bush. The freeze had killed all the others.

2. My _____*preference*_____ is strawberry ice cream, but no one else in the family likes it.

3. Much of California's economy is _____*dependent*_____ upon agriculture.

4. Considering that the criminal's <u>conscience</u> hasn't bothered him at all, I feel the great punishment was _____*suitable*_____.

5. My grandmother can use the money, but her _____*principal*_____ reason for working is to be with other people.

Now check your answers by turning to page 146. Fix any mistakes and fill in any blank spaces by writing in the correct answers. By doing so, you will complete this introduction to the five words.

You're now ready to strengthen your knowledge of the words you already know and to master the words you're only half sure of, or don't know at all. Turn to the next page.

Five Words in Context

Figure out the meanings of the following five words by looking *closely and carefully* at the sentences below. Doing so will prepare you for the matching test and practices that follow.

1 **dependent**
(di-pen'-dənt)
-*adjective*

   a. Some animals can take care of themselves shortly after birth, but human babies are **dependent** on their parents for years.

   b. Frank's father <u>counseled</u> him, "You are still much too **dependent** on me. It's about time you got a job and supported yourself."

2 **preference**
(pref'-ər-əns)
-*noun*

   a. There are Chinese, Italian, and Indian restaurants nearby. What's your **preference** for dinner tonight?

   b. What is your color **preference** for the living room? Cool blues and greens or warm oranges and yellows?

3 **principal**
(prin'-sə-pəl)
-*adjective*

   a. The speaker said the **principal** cause of success is hard work, not luck or talent.

   b. The Queen of England has no real power. The **principal** leader there is the prime minister.

4 **solitary**
(sol'-i-ter'-ē)
-*adjective*

   a. Patty decided she disliked the **solitary** life in her own apartment, so she started looking for a roommate.

   b. The sky was clear except for a **solitary** cloud directly overhead.

5 **suitable**
(soo'-tə-bəl)
-*adjective*

   a. Sharon asked her mother if her blue dress was **suitable** for a funeral, or if she had to wear black.

   b. We decided that the Red Lion restaurant would be **suitable** for our bowling banquet.

Matching Words and Definitions

Check your understanding of the five words by matching each word with its definition. Look above at the sentences in "Five Words in Context" as needed to decide on the meaning of each word.

_c_	1. **dependent**	a. choice; first choice; something preferred
_a_	2. **preference**	b. most important; chief; main
_b_	3. **principal**	c. relying on others for aid or support
_e_	4. **solitary**	d. right for a certain purpose; proper; acceptable
_d_	5. **suitable**	e. lonely, or lacking in companionship; single

➤ *Check 1*

Complete each sentence below with the correct word from the box. Use each word once.

dependent	preference	principal
solitary	suitable	

1. Jeans and tennis shoes are not _____*suitable*_____ for that fancy French restaurant.
2. What is your _____*preference*_____ in ice cream flavors? Most people prefer vanilla.
3. Instead of saying "the main reason," you can say "the _____*principal*_____ reason."
4. Babies are _____*dependent*_____ upon their parents for all their basic needs.
5. A _____*solitary*_____ life is a lonely life; a _____*solitary*_____ cloud is one that is all by itself.

Now check your answers to these questions by turning to page 146. Going over the answers carefully will help you prepare for the next three practices, for which answers are not given.

➤ *Check 2*

Complete each sentence below with the correct word from the box. Use each word once.

dependent	preference	principal
solitary	suitable	

1. My _____*preference*_____ is for a daytime job, but I would take a night shift if necessary.
2. I know you have several reasons for going to school, but what is the _____*principal*_____ reason?
3. My neighbors are looking for _____*suitable*_____ homes for the eight beautiful puppies their collie gave birth to last month.
4. Sometimes Nora felt like giving up, but she knew she couldn't because she had three young children and an elderly mother who were _____*dependent*_____ on her.
5. For two years, Henry David Thoreau lived alone in a shack near Walden Pond. He wrote about nature and his _____*solitary*_____ lifestyle in his book *Walden*.

➤ *Check 3*

Circle **C** if the italicized word is used **correctly**. Circle **I** if the word is used **incorrectly**.

Ⓒ I 1. The *principal* person in a band is its leader.

Ⓒ I 2. My blind uncle is *dependent* on his Seeing Eye dog.

C Ⓘ 3. When my son was little, tomatoes were his *preference*. They made him gag.

Ⓒ I 4. Use only plastic and glass in your microwave oven. Metal containers are not *suitable* for microwaves.

C Ⓘ 5. The *solitary* cars were so crowded in the parking lot that nobody could drive away until the cars behind them left.

➤ *Final Check:* Helpful Robots

Read the following passage carefully. Then fill in each blank with a different word from the box. (Context clues will help you figure out which word goes in which blank.)

dependent	preference	principal
solitary	suitable	

Until now, pizza-making was not considered a (1)_____*suitable*_____ job for persons with certain physical disabilities. But a new robot—the "Pizzabot"—can transform pizza restaurants into places that welcome disabled employees. The robot's (2)_____*principal*_____ advantage to the disabled is that it is voice-activated, meaning that a human can tell it what to do, and it will obey. Thus a disabled employee can take a telephone order and tell the Pizzabot the customer's (3)_____*preference*_____—a medium pizza with pepperoni, for example. The Pizzabot then tops a prepared crust with tomato sauce, sprinkles on the cheese and other toppings, and puts the pizza into the oven. Later, another human employee takes it out and serves it. The Pizzabot thus helps disabled people in two ways. First, they are less (4)_____*dependent*_____ on others for their support. Secondly, they spend time working with other people, rather than living a more (5)_____*solitary*_____ existence. The Pizzabot has another advantage, too—it never nibbles.

SCORES:	Check 2 _____ %	Check 3 _____ %	**Final Check** _____ %

Enter your scores above and in the vocabulary performance chart on the inside back cover of the book.

UNIT THREE: Test 1

PART A
Complete each sentence with a word from the box. Use each word once.

accompany	interpret	potential	principal	pursue
solitary	surplus	transform	transparent	wholesome

1. Every time Robert takes a girl out, he thinks about whether she has the
   _____*potential*_____ to be a good wife.

2. If glass bathtub doors weren't _____*transparent*_____, people would have more privacy in the tub.

3. A heavy spring rain _____*transform*_____(e)d our brown, flat lawn into a green carpet.

4. To _____*pursue*_____ a career, you often must get the proper education.

5. Playing outdoors for hours is more _____*wholesome*_____ than watching TV for hours.

6. Please donate your _____*surplus*_____ winter jackets and coats to the homeless.

7. Larry was afraid he'd feel too weak to drive himself home after having his teeth pulled, so he asked a friend to _____*accompany*_____ him.

8. Preferring a _____*solitary*_____ life, the scientist spent many years living and working alone in the desert.

9. Lena and Jack have many problems, but their _____*principal*_____ one seems to be that they don't discuss their feelings enough with each other.

10. I'm not sure how to _____*interpret*_____ Al's comment that my new outfit looks "like a rainbow." Did he mean it's pretty or that it makes me look like the tail end of a storm?

(Continues on next page)

PART B
Circle **C** if the italicized word is used **correctly**. Circle **I** if the word is used **incorrectly**.

Ⓒ I 11. On the morning of her wedding, Karen was happy to *detect* a little ray of sunshine peeking through the clouds.

Ⓒ I 12. It's sad that some people are more *fertile* than they want to be while others can't have any children.

C Ⓘ 13. The five-year-old girl was so *dependent* that she even made her bed and oatmeal by herself.

C Ⓘ 14. Everything about the Rands was *peculiar*—they were your ordinary American family.

Ⓒ I 15. What was meant to be a simple night at the movies was *complicated* by a flat tire and a storm.

C Ⓘ 16. The *ultimate* job in a successful business career might be running errands in a large office.

C Ⓘ 17. I was so happy at Kelly's *rejection* that the only thing I could think of all week was our date that weekend.

Ⓒ I 18. I *proposed* that the Park Board buy some new swings, but the treasurer said there wasn't enough money.

Ⓒ I 19. Because her husband was sick and couldn't work, Caren *appealed* to their landlady for extra time to pay the rent.

C Ⓘ 20. Nothing is more *suitable* for a job interview than torn jeans, dirty tennis shoes, unwashed hair, and cigarette breath.

Ⓒ I 21. My boss prefers to put more *emphasis* on pleasing customers than on making as many sales as possible in a day.

Ⓒ I 22. Laurie had only a *vague* idea about how to change a tire on her car, so she decided to learn exactly how before going away to college.

C Ⓘ 23. In green areas, there are about 50,000 spiders per acre. These *scarce* creatures help the balance of nature by eating numerous insects.

C Ⓘ 24. Many citizens were angry when the beautiful old courthouse was *established* in order to make room for an ugly, new shopping center.

Ⓒ I 25. The old "cliff-hanger" serials shown in movie houses got their name from the practice of leaving the hero at the end of each episode in a *desperate* situation—such as hanging from a cliff.

> **SCORE:** (Number correct) _____ x 4 = _____ %

Enter your score above and in the vocabulary performance chart on the inside back cover of the book.

UNIT THREE: *Test 2*

PART A: Synonyms

In the space provided, write the letter of the choice that is most nearly the **same** in meaning as the boldfaced word.

_b_ 1. **to transform**   **a)** build   **b)** change   **c)** make difficult   **d)** cross

_a_ 2. **to pursue**   **a)** follow   **b)** run from   **c)** suggest   **d)** create

_b_ 3. **to accompany**   **a)** avoid   **b)** go with   **c)** invite   **d)** visit

_c_ 4. **to propose**   **a)** aim for   **b)** ignore   **c)** suggest   **d)** be proper

_a_ 5. **an emphasis**   **a)** special attention   **b)** possibility
c) lack of importance   **d)** answer

_b_ 6. **a surplus**   **a)** subtraction   **b)** extra   **c)** a lot   **d)** answer

_a_ 7. **to detect**   **a)** discover   **b)** make   **c)** follow   **d)** commit a crime

_b_ 8. **a potential**   **a)** favorite   **b)** possibility   **c)** refusal   **d)** desire

_d_ 9. **a conscience**   **a)** awareness   **b)** rule   **c)** agreement   **d)** moral sense

_b_ 10. **to interpret**   **a)** notice   **b)** explain   **c)** chase   **d)** enter

_d_ 11. **a variety**   **a)** interest   **b)** health   **c)** leftover   **d)** assortment

_a_ 12. **a challenge**   **a)** something demanding   **b)** first choice   **c)** importance
d) change

_c_ 13. **to counsel**   **a)** meet   **b)** elect   **c)** give advice to   **d)** attract

(Continues on next page)

PART B: Antonyms
In the space provided, write the letter of the choice that is most nearly the **opposite** in meaning to the boldfaced word.

_a_ 14. **ultimate**   a) least   b) greatest   c) oldest   d) unknown

_d_ 15. **establish**   a) notice   b) recognize   c) hide   d) destroy

_a_ 16. **vague**   a) clear   b) healthy   c) weak   d) normal

_d_ 17. **peculiar**   a) serious   b) independent   c) unimportant
d) normal

_b_ 18. **scarce**   a) helpful   b) common   c) inexpensive
d) clear

_c_ 19. **fertile**   a) extra   b) main   c) not fruitful   d) most important

_d_ 20. **solitary**   a) usual   b) incorrect   c) immoral   d) with others

_b_ 21. **principal**   a) unhappy   b) least important   c) not famous
d) greatest

_b_ 22. **wholesome**   a) detailed   b) unhealthy   c) not busy   d) forgotten

_c_ 23. **to complicate**   a) destroy   b) leave   c) make simple   d) disapprove

_b_ 24. **dependent**   a) indirect   b) independent   c) uncommon
d) simple

_c_ 25. **a preference**   a) favorite   b) assortment   c) dislike   d) worry

---

SCORE: (Number correct) _____ x 4 = _____ %

Enter your score above and in the vocabulary performance chart on the inside back cover of the book.

Unit Four

19

Previewing the Words

Find out how many of the five words in this chapter you already know. Try to complete each sentence with the most suitable word from the list below. Use each word once.

Leave a sentence blank rather than guessing at an answer. Your purpose here is just to get a sense of the five words and what you may know about them.

aggravate	**cease**	**humane**
interference	**obnoxious**	

1. Are dress codes an unnecessary _____*interference*_____ in students' right to dress as they please?

2. It _____*aggravate*_____s my English teacher when students chew gum in class.

3. We had to wait for Neil to _____*cease*_____ practicing his drums before we could listen to the stereo.

4. The family considered it more _____*humane*_____ to have their dog painlessly "put to sleep" than to let him suffer through a long, painful death.

5. The loud, distasteful comments of the man behind me at the movie theater were so _____*obnoxious*_____ that I moved to an empty seat a few rows up.

Now check your answers by turning to page 146. Fix any mistakes and fill in any blank spaces by writing in the correct answers. By doing so, you will complete this introduction to the five words.

You're now ready to strengthen your knowledge of the words you already know and to master the words you're only half sure of, or don't know at all. Turn to the next page.

Five Words in Context

Figure out the meanings of the following five words by looking *closely and carefully* at the sentences below. Doing so will prepare you for the matching test and practices that follow.

1 **aggravate**
(ag'-rə-vāt)
-*verb*

    a. Mr. Benson **aggravates** his neighbors by walking his dog on their lawns.

    b. You will **aggravate** your sprained ankle if you walk on it.

2 **cease**
(sēs)
-*verb*

    a. Only after a court order did my neighbor **cease** burning trash in his back yard.

    b. When the snow finally **ceased** falling, we went out to shovel the driveway.

3 **humane**
(hyōō-mān')
adjective

    a. Children were afraid of the old lady living in the run-down house. The truth was, however, that she was very **humane,** too kind and gentle to hurt anyone.

    b. For years, many mentally retarded people were poorly treated in large institutions. Now many receive more **humane** care in small group homes.

4 **interference**
(in'-tər-fēr'-əns)
-*noun*

    a. When our microwave is on, it causes an **interference** in our TV picture. White lines run across the television screen until the microwave is off again.

    b. I love my mother-in-law, but her **interference** in arguments between my wife and me has got to stop.

5 **obnoxious**
(əb-nok'-shəs)
-*adjective*

    a. Children visiting the chicken farm held their noses to avoid the **obnoxious** smell.

    b. I won't go to Ramon's party if that **obnoxious** Lester will be there. He constantly insults and makes fun of people.

Matching Words and Definitions

Check your understanding of the five words by matching each word with its definition. Look above at the sentences in "Five Words in Context" as needed to decide on the meaning of each word.

  b   1. **aggravate**   a. gentle, kind, and sympathetic

  e   2. **cease**   b. to annoy; to make worse

  a   3. **humane**   c. getting in the way; taking part in other people's concerns

  c   4. **interference**   d. very unpleasant; disgusting

  d   5. **obnoxious**   e. to stop; discontinue

➤ *Check 1*

Complete each sentence below with the correct word from the box. Use each word once.

aggravate	**cease**	**humane**
interference	**obnoxious**	

1. _____*Interference*_____ in other people's lives appeals to those who don't like to mind their own business.

2. The **opposite** of "to begin" is "to _____*cease*_____."

3. _____*Humane*_____ people have some of the best human qualities.

4. Why is the taste of garlic so pleasant, yet the smell of garlic on our breath is sometimes so _____*obnoxious*_____?

5. Two meanings of "_____*aggravate*_____" are "to bother someone" and "to make (a problem of some kind) worse."

Now check your answers to these questions by turning to page 146. Going over the answers carefully will help you prepare for the next three practices, for which answers are not given.

➤ *Check 2*

Complete each sentence below with the correct word from the box. Use each word once.

aggravate	**cease**	**humane**
interference	**obnoxious**	

1. Some adults feel slurping with straws is _____*obnoxious*_____, but kids don't find it disgusting at all.

2. Sidney's parents threatened to _____*cease*_____ paying his college tuition if his grades didn't improve.

3. Even when insulted by prisoners, the guards are supposed to treat them in a(n) _____*humane*_____ manner.

4. Going to bed and taking it easy can actually _____*aggravate*_____ back pain. Gentle exercise is often more helpful.

5. Because of Mrs. Clyde's _____*interference*_____ in their affairs, her neighbors cross the street when they see her coming.

➤ *Check 3*

Circle **C** if the italicized word is used **correctly.** Circle **I** if the word is used **incorrectly.**

C (I) 1. When the weather was too dry, Indians performed rain dances to cause rain to *cease.*

(C) I 2. I admired the *humane* way in which the veterinarian treated the frightened animals.

(C) I 3. People who throw trash or cigarette butts out their car windows *aggravate* me.

C (I) 4. My parents welcomed my part-time job as an important *interference* in my learning to take responsibility.

C (I) 5. The sweet smell of the air after a spring rain is even more *obnoxious* than the odor of baking bread.

➤ *Final Check:* My Annoying Kid Brother

Read the following passage carefully. Then fill in each blank with a different word from the box. (Context clues will help you figure out which word goes in which blank.)

aggravate	**cease**	**humane**
interference	**obnoxious**	

My 12-year-old brother, Ozzie, is the most (1)_____*obnoxious*_____ kid I have ever known. His <u>principal</u> form of daily entertainment seems to be to (2)_____*aggravate*_____ me. He often squirts me with his water gun while I'm putting on my eye makeup. Sometimes he comes up behind me and screeches in my ears. Most of all, I hate his (3)_____*interference*_____ in my social life. If I'm on the phone with a friend, he listens in on the downstairs phone. As soon as we are talking about something serious, he starts making rude noises. Also, he reads my diary and then tells my boyfriend everything I have written about him. I have trouble treating Ozzie in a(n) (4)_____*humane*_____ way—I feel like killing him sometimes. I often ask myself, "Will his childish behavior ever (5)_____*cease*_____ ?" Maybe the only <u>remedy</u> for his behavior is growing up.

SCORES: Check 2 _____ %   Check 3 _____ %   **Final Check** _____ %

Enter your scores above and in the vocabulary performance chart on the inside back cover of the book.

20

Previewing the Words

Find out how many of the five words in this chapter you already know. Try to complete each sentence with the most suitable word from the list below. Use each word once.

Leave a sentence blank rather than guessing at an answer. Your purpose here is just to get a sense of the five words and what you may know about them.

analyze	**category**	**critical**
deliberate	**frustration**	

1. My aunt is _____*critical*_____ of her neighbors because they bought a pool and a new car, but didn't paint or fix up their house.

2. The young mother felt great _____*frustration*_____ when she wasn't allowed to hold her newborn baby because he was too tiny and sick.

3. When Ray plays quiz games with his friends, he answers more questions in the

   sports _____*category*_____ than anyone else.

4. Ellen wants to learn how to _____*analyze*_____ handwriting. She believes it's possible to <u>detect</u> a lot about people by studying the way they write.

5. When the boy next door broke our window, I didn't let it <u>aggravate</u> me because I thought it was an accident. When I found out his action was

   _____*deliberate*_____, I became very angry.

Now check your answers by turning to page 146. Fix any mistakes and fill in any blank spaces by writing in the correct answers. By doing so, you will complete this introduction to the five words.

You're now ready to strengthen your knowledge of the words you already know and to master the words you're only half sure of, or don't know at all. Turn to the next page.

Five Words in Context

Figure out the meanings of the following five words by looking *closely and carefully* at the sentences below. Doing so will prepare you for the matching test and practices that follow.

1 **analyze**
(an'-ə-līz)
-*verb*

a. Someone in the laboratory will **analyze** the blood sample.

b. Before we can suggest <u>suitable</u> solutions, we must carefully **analyze** the city's financial problems.

2 **category**
(kat'-ə-gōr'-ē)
-*noun*

a. When I was in high school, I didn't seem to fit into any **category**. I wasn't an athlete, a scholar, or a rebel.

b. The small store had many rock and blues records, but not much in the **categories** of classical and country music.

3 **critical**
(krit'-i-kəl)
-*adjective*

a. While my boss can be very **critical** when I don't do my best work, she's also quick to praise me when I do well.

b. One secretary at our office is so **critical** of herself that she even blames herself for other people's mistakes.

4 **deliberate**
(di-lib'-ər-it)
-*adjective*

a. Our company has taken **deliberate** steps to improve safety conditions for all workers.

b. Mike didn't bump into me by accident. His push was **deliberate**.

5 **frustration**
(frus-trā'-shən)
-*noun*

a. Elaine felt great **frustration** because she had practiced hard to pass her driver's test, but had failed it for the third time.

b. After fouling out in the third quarter of the championship game, Sandra's **frustration** was so great that she felt like quitting basketball.

Matching Words and Definitions

Check your understanding of the five words by matching each word with its definition. Look above at the sentences in "Five Words in Context" as needed to decide on the meaning of each word.

  c   1. **analyze**

  e   2. **category**

  a   3. **critical**

  b   4. **deliberate**

  d   5. **frustration**

a. disapproving; tending to find fault

b. carefully planned; done on purpose

c. to examine carefully; to study

d. disappointment; discouragement

e. a group of people or things considered to have something in common; a type

➤ Check 1

Complete each sentence below with the correct word from the box. Use each word once.

analyze	**category**	**critical**
deliberate	**frustration**	

1. Which _____*category*_____ of music do you prefer, rock or country?
2. To _____*analyze*_____ a blood sample, look at it under a microscope.
3. A planned action is _____*deliberate*_____.
4. When your boss finds fault with what you've done, he is being _____*critical*_____ of you.
5. To avoid the _____*frustration*_____ of failing the driving test again, Elaine decided to take driving lessons.

Now check your answers to these questions by turning to page 146. Going over the answers carefully will help you prepare for the next three practices, for which answers are not given.

➤ Check 2

Complete each sentence below with the correct word from the box. Use each word once.

analyze	**category**	**critical**
deliberate	**frustration**	

1. Because of his _____*frustration*_____ at being laid off from work, my brother often yells at his wife and children.
2. Ivy rarely finds fault with herself, but she is _____*critical*_____ of her friends even when they make a small mistake.
3. After several people in the household became ill, they had their water supply _____*analyze*_____d to see if it contained anything harmful.
4. To plan our budget, we've organized our expenses into groups. For example, one _____*category*_____ is home costs, and another is car expenses.
5. When Paul wiped his muddy boots on the new carpet, it was _____*deliberate*_____. He wanted to see if the carpeting was as easy to clean as the saleswoman had said.

➣Check 3

Circle the letter of the best answer to each question.

1. To *analyze* something, you should a. avoid it   (b.) inspect it   c. admire it
2. One *category* of books is   a. bookmarks   (b.) children's books   c. bookstores
3. The **opposite** of *critical* is   a. skillful   (b.) approving   c. brave
4. The **opposite** of *deliberate* is   a. curious   b. generous   (c.) accidental
5. The **opposite** of *frustration* is   (a.) satisfaction   b. pain   c. honesty

➣*Final Check:* Barry's Job Evaluation

Read the following passage carefully. Then fill in each blank with a different word from the box. (Context clues will help you figure out which word goes in which blank.)

analyze	category	critical
deliberate	frustration	

When Barry began working in an auto parts store, he was told that during the first month his boss, Mr. Kelly, would (1)_____*analyze*_____ his work and write a report on how he was doing. If Barry's report was good, he could keep the job. If not, he would lose it. The report would be divided into two kinds of skills. The first (2)_____*category*_____ was technical skills, such as running the cash register and advising customers on auto parts. The second type was personal skills, including being respectful to customers and coming to work on time.

In the report, Mr. Kelly was (3)_____*critical*_____ of the way Barry spoke to customers. Mr. Kelly said he understood the (4)_____*frustration*_____ of dealing with people who were obnoxious or hard to please. However, workers had to be patient and polite at all times. The boss was happy with Barry's work in other areas. He said that as long as Barry improved the way he treated customers, he could keep his job. After that, Barry made a (5)_____*deliberate*_____ effort to remain calm and helpful to even the most annoying of customers. In time, showing patience became almost second nature to him.

| *SCORES:* | Check 2 _____ % | Check 3 _____ % | Final Check _____ % |

Enter your scores above and in the vocabulary performance chart on the inside back cover of the book.

21

Previewing the Words

Find out how many of the five words in this chapter you already know. Try to complete each sentence with the most suitable word from the list below. Use each word once.

Leave a sentence blank rather than guessing at an answer. Your purpose here is just to get a sense of the five words and what you may know about them.

abundant	**demonstrate**	**distinct**
exaggerate	**reduction**	

1. It seems everyone who runs for public office promises a(n) _____*reduction*_____ in taxes, but the winner always ends up raising taxes.

2. I don't know why people get the Thompson twins mixed up. I can see _____*distinct*_____ differences in their features.

3. We had such a(n) _____*abundant*_____ supply of firewood this year that we had <u>surplus</u> wood to give to our neighbor.

4. I have two old movies that _____*demonstrate*_____ the talents of W.C. Fields; they show why he's considered a comic genius.

5. Zena thought I _____*exaggerate*_____(e)d when I said my brother is seven feet tall, but when she met him, she saw I wasn't stretching the truth.

Now check your answers by turning to page 146. Fix any mistakes and fill in any blank spaces by writing in the correct answers. By doing so, you will complete this introduction to the five words.

You're now ready to strengthen your knowledge of the words you already know and to master the words you're only half sure of, or don't know at all. Turn to the next page.

Five Words in Context

Figure out the meanings of the following five words by looking *closely and carefully* at the sentences below. Doing so will prepare you for the matching test and practices that follow.

1 **abundant**
(ə-bun'-dənt)
-*adjective*

    a. Our apple tree was especially <u>fertile</u> this year. It bore such an **abundant** crop that we'll have plenty of applesauce all winter.

    b. Although Mrs. Richards is almost 70, her energy is so **abundant** that she tires out her grandchildren when she plays with them.

2 **demonstrate**
(dem'-ən-strāt')
-*verb*

    a. When I asked the salesman to **demonstrate** the camera, it was clear he didn't know how to use it.

    b. Please **demonstrate** the proper way to fold the flag so that our new members will understand how to do it.

3 **distinct**
(di-stingkt')
-*adjective*

    a. Since the photo is not **distinct**, we couldn't recognize anyone in it.

    b. At the store, I thought the jacket and pants matched, but when I got them home, I saw a **distinct** difference in their colors.

4 **exaggerate**
(ig-zaj'-ə-rāt')
-*verb*

    a. Mother, reminding us not to stretch the truth, used to joke, "I've told you a million times never to **exaggerate**!"

    b. I don't **exaggerate** about Randall's musical ability; he really is an excellent guitarist.

5 **reduction**
(ri-duk'-shən)
-*noun*

    a. Great Aunt Elsie has experienced a **reduction** in height. She used to be 5 feet 7 inches, and now she's only 5 feet 6.

    b. When our company offered to pay workers for sick days they didn't use, there was a sudden **reduction** in the amount of sick time taken.

Matching Words and Definitions

Check your understanding of the five words by matching each word with its definition. Look above at the sentences in "Five Words in Context" as needed to decide on the meaning of each word.

   _b_   1. **abundant**   a. clear; obvious

   _e_   2. **demonstrate**   b. very plentiful; more than enough

   _a_   3. **distinct**   c. to state that something is greater in some way than it really is; overstate

   _c_   4. **exaggerate**   d. a decrease

   _d_   5. **reduction**   e. to explain or teach by showing

➤ *Check 1*

Complete each sentence below with the correct word from the box. Use each word once.

abundant	demonstrate	distinct
exaggerate	reduction	

1. The **opposite** of an increase in pay is a _____*reduction*_____ in pay.
2. The **opposite** of a supply that is too small is a(n) _____*abundant*_____ supply.
3. The **opposite** of understating a fact is to _____*exaggerate*_____ it.
4. The **opposite** of an unclear memory is a(n) _____*distinct*_____ one.
5. The uncooperative salesperson refused to _____*demonstrate*_____ to me how to use the VCR.

Now check your answers to these questions by turning to page 146. Going over the answers carefully will help you prepare for the next three practices, for which answers are not given.

➤ *Check 2*

Complete each sentence below with the correct word from the box. Use each word once.

abundant	demonstrate	distinct
exaggerate	reduction	

1. You may have forgotten, but I have the _____*distinct*_____ memory that you promised to take me to dinner tonight.
2. The _____*abundant*_____ rains were too much of a good thing—they actually ruined some crops.
3. Doris always says she earns more tips than the other waitresses, but they think she _____*exaggerate*_____s about how much she makes.
4. Despite the business slowdown, there will be no _____*reduction*_____ of workers at our company. Our <u>humane</u> boss prefers not to lay anybody off.
5. When Joy's husband said he "didn't know how" to do laundry, she took him to the basement and _____*demonstrate*_____(e)d just how the washing machine worked.

➤ *Check 3*

Circle **C** if the italicized word is used **correctly.** Circle **I** if the word is used **incorrectly.**

Ⓒ I   1. The teacher in beauty school *demonstrated* how to make French braids.

C Ⓘ 2. The flavor of the mint in the vegetable stew was so *distinct* that I didn't even notice it.

C Ⓘ 3. The farmers' hay crop was *abundant*. They had barely enough to feed the animals.

Ⓒ I   4. There was a *reduction* in the price of the house because of termite damage.

C Ⓘ 5. The firefighter who rescued a child *exaggerated* his bravery, saying, "Anyone would have done the same."

➤ *Final Check:* The Vacuum Cleaner Salesman

Read the following passage carefully. Then fill in each blank with a different word from the box. (Context clues will help you figure out which word goes in which blank.)

abundant	demonstrate	distinct
exaggerate	reduction	

I'll never forget the day a salesman (1)_____*demonstrate*_____d his vacuum cleaner on my living room rug. I know some salespeople (2)_____*exaggerate*_____ their product's good qualities, so I didn't believe everything he said. But I let him show me what his machine could do.

The first thing he did was deliberately wipe his muddy feet on my rug. Next, he dumped a(n) (3)_____*abundant*_____ amount of ashes onto it. Then he vacuumed the mess up. In no time, there was a difference between the rest of the rug and the part he had dirtied and then cleaned. A clear light stripe now ran down the middle of my rug. The machine was great. He told me how lucky I was to have the chance to buy it then because of a great (4)_____*reduction*_____ in the price. Sadly, I had to tell him that even the lower price was too high for me. When he started to leave, I asked him to finish cleaning the carpet. But he said the only part of the rug he had to clean was the section he had dirtied. He had done that, as I could plainly see.

I'm reminded of the frustrations of that day every time I walk through my living room. It still has a(n) (5)_____*distinct*_____ light stripe right down the middle.

SCORES:	Check 2 _____ %	Check 3 _____ %	Final Check _____ %

Previewing the Words

Find out how many of the five words in this chapter you already know. Try to complete each sentence with the most suitable word from the list below. Use each word once.

Leave a sentence blank rather than guessing at an answer. Your purpose here is just to get a sense of the five words and what you may know about them.

anticipate	**linger**	**miserable**
reluctant	**specific**	

1. I _____*anticipate*_____ about forty guests at our New Year's Eve party, but I'm preparing food for fifty, just in case.

2. Jay was _____*miserable*_____ when he lost the basketball game for his team.

3. Although the apartment met our needs, we were _____*reluctant*_____ to sign a long-term lease.

4. Could you _____*linger*_____ for a few minutes after the meeting so I can talk privately to you?

5. Because Clark's directions were so _____*specific*_____, I found his new home without difficulty.

Now check your answers by turning to page 146. Fix any mistakes and fill in any blank spaces by writing in the correct answers. By doing so, you will complete this introduction to the five words.

You're now ready to strengthen your knowledge of the words you already know and to master the words you're only half sure of, or don't know at all. Turn to the next page.

Five Words in Context

Figure out the meanings of the following five words by looking *closely and carefully* at the sentences below. Doing so will prepare you for the matching test and practices that follow.

1 **anticipate**
(an-tis'-ə-pāt')
-verb

 a. Rod **anticipated** heavy traffic this morning, so he left for the airport an hour early.

 b. The children **anticipate** Christmas more than any of the other holidays.

2 **linger**
(ling'-gər)
-verb

 a. My husband has difficulty leaving any social event. He **lingers** by the door, chatting with our hosts for ages.

 b. After the bowling matches are over, we like to **linger** for a while to talk to our friends on the other teams.

3 **miserable**
(miz'-ər-ə-həl)
-adjective

 a. The Farrells were **miserable** on their camping trip because the black flies wouldn't <u>cease</u> biting them for a minute.

 b. I was disturbed when I read of the **miserable** conditions in many refugee camps.

4 **reluctant**
(ri-luk'-tənt)
-adjective

 a. Since I'm **reluctant** to have people know my phone number, I keep it unlisted.

 b. Although the lawyer was **reluctant** to tell his client such disappointing news, he had no choice but to do so.

5 **specific**
(spi-sif'-ik)
-adjective

 a. Gina said that she and Howard had some sort of quarrel, but she didn't tell me the **specific** details.

 b. I give very **specific** instructions to new babysitters so they'll understand exactly what I want done. I even <u>demonstrate</u> how to diaper and feed my son.

Matching Words and Definitions

Check your understanding of the five words by matching each word with its definition. Look above at the sentences in "Five Words in Context" as needed to decide on the meaning of each word.

_c_	1. **anticipate**	a. unwilling; hesitating to do something one is opposed to
_b_	2. **linger**	b. to remain, especially as if unwilling to leave; to hang around
_e_	3. **miserable**	c. to expect; to look forward to with pleasure
_a_	4. **reluctant**	d. definite; exact
_d_	5. **specific**	e. very unhappy or uncomfortable; causing suffering

➤ Check 1

Complete each sentence below with the correct word from the box. Use each word once.

anticipate	linger	miserable
reluctant	specific	

1. A person might _____*linger*_____ at a party, but not in jail. Who would hang around jail on purpose?

2. To make the directions to your new house clear, be as _____*specific*_____ as possible.

3. We were _____*reluctant*_____ to sign a long-term lease for the apartment in case we found another one we liked better.

4. Two very different meanings of "_____*anticipate*_____" are "to predict a future situation" (for example, to expect heavy traffic on the way to the airport) and "to look to a future event with pleasure" (for example, to look forward to Christmas).

5. If we say *someone* feels _____*miserable*_____, we mean he or she is *feeling* sad or suffering. If we say that *something* is _____*miserable*_____, we may mean that it *causes* unhappiness or suffering.

Now check your answers to these questions by turning to page 146. Going over the answers carefully will help you prepare for the next three practices, for which answers are not given.

➤ Check 2

Complete each sentence below with the correct word from the box. Use each word once.

anticipate	linger	miserable
reluctant	specific	

1. Gino is sure to be _____*miserable*_____ if he doesn't get shots during the allergy season.

2. The Wallaces _____*anticipate*_____ a happy reunion with their family in Ohio. They especially look forward to seeing their cousins again.

3. After dinner at the restaurant, we didn't _____*linger*_____ with our coffee because there was a long line of people waiting for a table.

4. I wish my girlfriend would give me a more _____*specific*_____ answer than "something fun" when I ask what she'd like to do on the weekend.

5. Many celebrities are _____*reluctant*_____ to admit their ages. Some are <u>vague</u> when asked how old they are ("Old enough"), while others simply lie.

➤ *Check 3*

Circle the letter of the best answer to each question.

1. To *anticipate* means
   a. to remember   ⓑ to look forward to
   c. to hang around

2. We could describe as *miserable* someone who
   ⓐ has a toothache   b. is surprised   c. is unwilling

3. People might *linger* at a
   a. dentist's office   b. voting booth   ⓒ friend's house

4. Many children are *reluctant* to eat   a. at any time   ⓑ spinach   c. ice cream

5. The most *specific* directions are: a. on Oak St.   b. on Oak St. near 1st Ave.
   ⓒ at 55 Oak St.

➤ *Final Check:* "Meet You at the Park!"

Read the following passage carefully. Then fill in each blank with a different word from the box. (Context clues will help you figure out which word goes in which blank.)

anticipate	linger	miserable
reluctant	specific	

"We'll meet you at the park!" Anita yelled as her kids piled into her car and mine scrambled into our station wagon. When my children and I reached the park, we found thousands of people, but not Anita's family. Since we had talked about going on the rides, we decided to wait for them near the ticket booth. They didn't show up, but we were (1)_____*reluctant*_____ to leave that spot in case they would come after we left. After a while, I let the kids search for them, and I (2)_____*linger*_____(e)d in the ticket booth area. Later, the kids came back alone; none of us had seen our friends.

We waited and waited some more, but they still didn't come. Since we hadn't (3)_____*anticipate*_____(e)d standing so long in the cool ocean breeze, we didn't bring sweaters. The longer we waited for them, and the colder we got, the more (4)_____*miserable*_____ we felt. I wished we had been more (5)_____*specific*_____ about our plans, saying something like, "I'll see you at the merry-go-round." As it turned out, we never did find them that evening.

SCORES:	Check 2 _____ %	Check 3 _____ %	Final Check _____ %

Enter your scores above and in the vocabulary performance chart on the inside back cover of the book.

Previewing the Words

Find out how many of the five words in this chapter you already know. Try to complete each sentence with the most suitable word from the list below. Use each word once.

Leave a sentence blank rather than guessing at an answer. Your purpose here is just to get a sense of the five words and what you may know about them.

artificial	**frequency**	**represent**
temporary	**triumph**	

1. The thorns on a rose are often used to _____*represent*_____ life's problems.

2. I don't like to see baseball played on _____*artificial*_____ turf. I prefer real grass.

3. Winning the election was a special _____*triumph*_____ for Jane Gimble because many had predicted she would lose.

4. VCRs and tape decks should be cleaned from time to time. The more they are used, the greater the _____*frequency*_____ of the cleaning should be.

5. Bev promised her stay in our apartment would be only _____*temporary*_____, and sure enough, she found a place of her own in just two days.

Now check your answers by turning to page 147. Fix any mistakes and fill in any blank spaces by writing in the correct answers. By doing so, you will complete this introduction to the five words.

You're now ready to strengthen your knowledge of the words you already know and to master the words you're only half sure of, or don't know at all. Turn to the next page.

Five Words in Context

Figure out the meanings of the following five words by looking *closely and carefully* at the sentences below. Doing so will prepare you for the matching test and practices that follow.

1 **artificial**
(är'-tə-fish'-əl)
-adjective

   a. My uncle, who lost his left arm in a tractor accident, was recently fitted for an **artificial** arm.

   b. Cary dislikes her boss so much that she can't even smile at him naturally. She gives him such an **artificial** smile that it looks like it's pasted on.

2 **frequency**
(frē'-kwən-sē)
-noun

   a. Mike and Adam used to visit each other once or twice a week, but the **frequency** of their visits has dropped since Adam got married.

   b. The **frequency** of television ads is so great that it makes me reluctant to watch movies on TV. I prefer to rent them and see them without all the interruptions.

3 **represent**
(rep'-ri-zent')
-verb

   a. Colors sometimes **represent** human qualities. For example, white often stands for innocence and yellow for lack of courage.

   b. Loretta was chosen to **represent** her class at the Student Council meetings.

4 **temporary**
(tem'-pə-rer'-ē)
-adjective

   a. My sister used a **temporary** hair color to dye her hair green just for St. Patrick's Day.

   b. A **temporary** worker will be hired until Kwan recovers from her injury.

5 **triumph**
(trī'-əmf)
-noun

   a. Our football team's **triumph** over the state's first-place team was the cause for a huge celebration.

   b. My brother's hard work, good teachers, and understanding parents led to his **triumph** over a learning disability.

Matching Words and Definitions

Check your understanding of the five words by matching each word with its definition. Look above at the sentences in "Five Words in Context" as needed to decide on the meaning of each word.

_e_	1. **artificial**	a.	how often something happens
_a_	2. **frequency**	b.	to be a symbol for; to act as an agent for
_b_	3. **represent**	c.	effective for a limited time only; serving for a limited time only
_c_	4. **temporary**	d.	a victory; a satisfying success
_d_	5. **triumph**	e.	not genuine or natural, but man-made; false, or pretended

➤ *Check 1*

Complete each sentence below with the correct word from the box. Use each word once.

artificial	frequency	represent
temporary	triumph	

1. Beating a first-place team is a bigger _____*triumph*_____ than winning over the last-place team.
2. Substitute teachers get _____*temporary*_____ assignments.
3. _____*Artificial*_____ things are often fake, like a false smile or plastic grass.
4. The _____*frequency*_____ of an event is the rate at which it happens.
5. Two meanings of "_____*represent*_____" are "to stand for" (for example, yellow stands for lack of courage) and "to speak on behalf of others" (for example, a member of Student Council speaks on behalf of her class.)

Now check your answers to these questions by turning to page 147. Going over the answers carefully will help you prepare for the next three practices, for which answers are not given.

➤ *Check 2*

Complete each sentence below with the correct word from the box. Use each word once.

artificial	frequency	represent
temporary	triumph	

1. Taylor's job was _____*temporary*_____. He was hired as an extra salesman in the store only for the Christmas season.
2. My new dress looks black under _____*artificial*_____ light, but dark blue in sunlight.
3. When a cure is found for AIDS, it will be one of the greatest medical _____*triumph*_____s of this century.
4. The _____*frequency*_____ of Aunt Alicia's visits has increased since she and I began working together on our family tree.
5. I disagree with our senator on so many things that I feel he doesn't truly _____*represent*_____ me in Congress.

➤Check 3

A. Circle the letter of the answer that means the **opposite** of the italicized word.

1. *artificial*   (a.)natural   b. cold   c. beautiful

2. *temporary*   a. nearby   b. young   (c.) unending

3. *triumph*   a. confusion   (b.)failure   c. delay

B. Circle C if the italicized word is used **correctly.** Circle I if the word is used **incorrectly.**

(C) I   4. The *frequency* of a sunset is once a day.

(C) I   5. The lion often *represents* courage.

➤*Final Check:* **An Unhappy Playboy**

Read the following passage carefully. Then fill in each blank with a different word from the box. (Context clues will help you figure out which word goes in which blank.)

artificial	frequency	represent
temporary	triumph	

Lloyd has had more romances than anyone I know. I don't <u>exaggerate</u> when I say he's got a new girl almost every time I see him. Sounds like fun, right? Wrong. He's one of the unhappiest people I've ever met. He doesn't <u>pursue</u> rich relationships. All that matters is the (1)_____*frequency*_____ with which he begins new ones—the more often, the better. In order to start new romances so often, each relationship must be very (2)_____*temporary*_____, no more than a few months. The way he pretends to adore each girl shows how (3) _____*artificial*_____ his affections really are.

Lloyd constantly needs new romantic (4)_____*triumph*_____s to feel good about himself. When I <u>analyze</u> his behavior, I wonder if it has something to do with the fact that his parents divorced when he was very young. He hardly knows either of them today. Maybe the constant "winning" of new women somehow (5)_____*represent*_____s to him winning the affection of the family he never had. Whatever his true needs are, I hope one day he'll become <u>conscious</u> of them and then change his behavior to a happier way of life.

SCORES:	**Check 2** _____ %	**Check 3** _____ %	**Final Check** _____ %

Enter your scores above and in the vocabulary performance chart on the inside back cover of the book.

Previewing the Words

Find out how many of the five words in this chapter you already know. Try to complete each sentence with the most suitable word from the list below. Use each word once.

Leave a sentence blank rather than guessing at an answer. Your purpose here is just to get a sense of the five words and what you may know about them.

coincide	**considerable**	**intentional**
unstable	**utilize**	

1. It's no wonder the vase fell over. It was so top-heavy with flowers that it was _____*unstable*_____.

2. There was a(n) _____*considerable*_____ amount of fog along the coast, so we had to drive slowly.

3. I didn't have to wait at all for my date at the restaurant. Her arrival there

   _____*coincide*_____ (e)d exactly with mine.

4. Marty is a creative jewelry designer. He _____*utilize*_____s old zipper tabs and electrical wires in his necklaces and earrings.

5. I know Karen ignored you at the party, but her rudeness wasn't

   _____*intentional*_____. She wasn't wearing her glasses and couldn't see you across the room.

Now check your answers by turning to page 147. Fix any mistakes and fill in any blank spaces by writing in the correct answers. By doing so, you will complete this introduction to the five words.

You're now ready to strengthen your knowledge of the words you already know and to master the words you're only half sure of, or don't know at all. Turn to the next page.

Five Words in Context

Figure out the meanings of the following five words by looking *closely and carefully* at the sentences below. Doing so will prepare you for the matching test and practices that follow.

1 **coincide**
(kō'-in-sīd')
-*verb*

   a. My best friend from high school and I have moved to different states. We try to make our visits to our hometown **coincide** so we can see each other.

   b. My friend's and my cousin's weddings are both on the same day. I wish they didn't **coincide** because I really want to go to both.

2 **considerable**
(kən-sid'-ər-ə-bəl)
-*adjective*

   a. After **considerable** effort, I finally found Tyrone's apartment.

   b. Elena spends a **considerable** amount of time caring for her pets each week, but she doesn't mind because she loves them.

3 **intentional**
(in ten' chə nəl)
-*adjective*

   a. The police believe the fire was **intentional,** but they don't know why someone would purposely burn down the library.

   b. The pitcher's four throws outside the batter's box were **intentional.** He wanted to make the good batter walk to first base so he couldn't hit a home run.

4 **unstable**
(un-stā'-bəl)
-*adjective*

   a. I was afraid to climb above the third step on the ladder because it felt **unstable.**

   b. Medication allows many otherwise **unstable** people to live normal lives at home, instead of living in mental institutions.

5 **utilize**
(yōōt'-l-īz')
-*verb*

   a. Old bread can be **utilized** to make croutons and bread crumbs.

   b. Cindy would love to get a job that **utilizes** her swimming ability—perhaps as a lifeguard or a swimming teacher.

Matching Words and Definitions

Check your understanding of the five words by matching each word with its definition. Look above at the sentences in "Five Words in Context" as needed to decide on the meaning of each word.

e	1. **coincide**	a.	done on purpose
c	2. **considerable**	b.	unsteady; not firmly fixed; not emotionally steady and reliable
a	3. **intentional**	c.	rather great or large
b	4. **unstable**	d.	to make use of; put to (good) use
d	5. **utilize**	e.	to happen at the same time

➤ *Check 1*

Complete each sentence below with the correct word from the box. Use each word once.

coincide	considerable	intentional
unstable	utilize	

1. The two weddings _____*coincide*_____d; that is, they took place on the same afternoon.

2. A _____*considerable*_____ amount of time is the opposite of a rather small amount of time.

3. The fire was started on purpose; in other words, it was _____*intentional*_____.

4. My brother is glad he'll be able to _____*utilize*_____ his mechanical skills in his new job.

5. A(n) _____*unstable*_____ *thing* is not physically steady. A(n) _____*unstable*_____ *person* may be mentally unsteady.

Now check your answers to these questions by turning to page 147. Going over the answers carefully will help you prepare for the next three practices, for which answers are not given.

➤ *Check 2*

Complete each sentence below with the correct word from the box. Use each word once.

coincide	considerable	intentional
unstable	utilize	

1. Let's plan our lunch breaks to _____*coincide*_____ so that we can meet for lunch.

2. My failure to pick you up on time was not _____*intentional*_____. A huge traffic accident made me late.

3. Lucas had a _____*considerable*_____ number of complaints about his vacation trip, but his wife thought the trip was just fine.

4. Mel was too _____*unstable*_____ to hold down a steady job. Some days he felt fine, but most days he was too nervous or confused to work.

5. I _____*utilize*_____d old broken pieces of <u>transparent</u> plastic to make the windows for my daughter's dollhouse.

➤ *Check 3*

Circle **C** if the italicized word is used **correctly.** Circle **I** if the word is used **incorrectly.**

Ⓒ I 1. My mother *utilizes* old bathroom towels for drying dishes.

C Ⓘ 2. My birthday—October 31—*coincides* with New Year's Eve.

Ⓒ I 3. The chair is *unstable* because one leg is shorter than the others.

C Ⓘ 4. The concert tickets only cost a *considerable* amount—one dollar per person.

C Ⓘ 5. Harold's snoring is *intentional*, of course. He'd love to stop if he could.

➤ *Final Check:* **A Bad Taste Party**

Read the following passage carefully. Then fill in each blank with a different word from the box. (Context clues will help you figure out which word goes in which blank.)

coincide	considerable	intentional
unstable	utilize	

When Lorie and I realized that our birthdays (1)____*coincide*____d, we decided to celebrate together. We put (2)____*considerable*____ thought into the theme of our party and came up with a terrific idea. We decided to host a "bad taste" party. At times, we all do something tasteless by accident, we reasoned. Why not make a time for (3)____*intentional*____ bad taste?

We began by sending out scribbled invitations that were barely legible. Our friends loved the idea, and the party was a great triumph. They came dressed as tastelessly as possible, wearing black fishnet stockings and loafers, mismatched plaid pants and striped shirts, and blinding color combinations. I filled vases with ugly artificial flowers and (4)____*utilize*____d my fancy wineglasses for serving lime Kool Aid. We were all having a great time when I noticed a normally-dressed couple staring at us. I realized they were our new neighbors, whom I had invited to drop by sometime. As I approached them in my too-tight neon-orange leotards and green false eyelashes, they backed away, no doubt thinking I was mentally (5)____*unstable*____. But I managed to explain what was going on, and they loved the idea too. They went home and returned a few minutes later dressed as tastelessly as the rest of us.

SCORES:	Check 2 _____ %	Check 3 _____ %	**Final Check** _____ %

Enter your scores above and in the vocabulary performance chart on the inside back cover of the book.

UNIT FOUR: Test 1

PART A
Complete each sentence with a word from the box. Use each word once.

aggravate	artificial	cease	coincide	deliberate
linger	reduction	reluctant	represent	unstable

1. Dave _____*linger*_____(e)d at the diner long after he had finished eating, hoping to find the courage to ask the waitress out.

2. When I saw the _____*reduction*_____ in my bank balance, I became worried because I hadn't taken any money out recently.

3. Don't you feel sorry for people whose birthdays _____*coincide*_____ with Christmas?

4. In the language of chemistry, "H_2O" _____*represent*_____s water.

5. My remarks seemed to _____*aggravate*_____ the angry man, making him even angrier.

6. The company claims that its cereal is all natural, with no _____*artificial*_____ ingredients at all.

7. After getting off of the roller coaster, Mel felt _____*unstable*_____, so he sat down until he felt steady again.

8. Nadia was _____*reluctant*_____ to meet me for lunch because she was low on money and didn't want to borrow any.

9. The local hardware store has _____*cease*_____(e)d selling wood. Those needing wood will now have to make the longer trip to the lumber yard.

10. Holly made a(n) _____*deliberate*_____ effort to get her brother into trouble. She pinched her arm till it was pink, and then told her parents that he did it.

(Continues on next page)

PART B
Circle C if the italicized word is used **correctly**. Circle I if the word is used **incorrectly**.

C I 11. After fighting in a pool of green Jello, the wrestlers looked *obnoxious*.

C I 12. Our town hired a traffic specialist to *analyze* our road and stoplight needs.

C I 13. Every week, the *humane* king sent dozens of innocent people to his cruel prisons.

C I 14. My parents and I argue over their *interference* in how I raise my children.

C I 15. The *frustration* of being on vacation, sleeping late, and waking up to a sunny day is wonderful.

C I 16. These peanut butter cookies use *abundant* flour. The recipe calls only for peanut butter, sugar, and eggs!

C I 17. Having been ill for two months during her senior year, Valerie felt that graduating was a *triumph* for her.

C I 18. The postmark was so *distinct* that I couldn't tell if the letter had come from New Hampshire or New Mexico.

C I 19. One man who is interested in recycling has *utilized* old tires to insulate the basement of his new home.

C I 20. We had only a *considerable* amount of snow this winter. The weather was so warm that it was mostly rain that fell.

C I 21. To *demonstrate* how a magnet works, the teacher spread iron bits over a piece of paper and then placed a magnet underneath.

C I 22. When you write essays, support your general points with *specific* examples.

C I 23. My sister and I laughed as we *anticipated* the time years ago when she felt someone's fur coat in an elevator and said, "Mommy, it's porcupine fur."

C I 24. My daughter's interest in piano lessons turned out to be more *temporary* than I expected. She continued them through high school and then became a piano teacher herself.

C I 25. I've divided my clothing into three *categories*: 1) clothes for now, 2) clothes for ten pounds ago, and 3) miracle clothes (it would be a miracle if I ever fit into them again).

> **SCORE:** (Number correct) _____ x 4 = _____ %

Enter your score above and in the vocabulary performance chart on the inside back cover of the book.

UNIT FOUR: Test 2

PART A: Synonyms
In the space provided, write the letter of the choice that is most nearly the **same** in meaning as the boldfaced word.

  _b_   1. **to exaggerate**   **a)** leave   **b)** overstate   **c)** worsen   **d)** ignore

  _b_   2. **to aggravate**   **a)** get together   **b)** worsen   **c)** win   **d)** expect

  _d_   3. **to demonstrate**   **a)** sell   **b)** give   **c)** harm   **d)** show

  _a_   4. **to analyze**   **a)** study   **b)** use   **c)** show   **d)** entertain

  _c_   5. **a category**   **a)** kindness   **b)** horror   **c)** type   **d)** assortment

  _a_   6. **distinct**   **a)** clear   **b)** far   **c)** helpful   **d)** loud

  _d_   7. **to represent**   **a)** give   **b)** expect   **c)** answer   **d)** be a symbol for

  _b_   8. **a frustration**   **a)** wish   **b)** disappointment   **c)** decrease   **d)** charity

  _d_   9. **to coincide**   **a)** pay   **b)** overstate   **c)** get in the way
                      d) happen together

  _c_ 10. **to anticipate**   **a)** battle   **b)** worsen   **c)** expect   **d)** free

  _d_ 11. **the frequency**   **a)** power   **b)** visit   **c)** victory   **d)** oftenness

  _c_ 12. **to utilize**   **a)** study   **b)** overstate   **c)** make use of
                      d) be a symbol for

  _b_ 13. **a triumph**   **a)** effort   **b)** success   **c)** battle   **d)** loss

(Continues on next page)

PART B: Antonyms

In the space provided, write the letter of the choice that is most nearly the **opposite** in meaning to the boldfaced word.

<u>b</u> 14. **miserable**   a) able   b) comfortable   c) expensive   d) small

<u>b</u> 15. **abundant**   a) found   b) rare   c) faraway   d) unimportant

<u>c</u> 16. **to cease**   a) lose   b) leave   c) continue   d) find

<u>c</u> 17. **humane**   a) dead   b) wild   c) cruel   d) alive

<u>a</u> 18. **reluctant**   a) willing   b) angry   c) active   d) not active

<u>c</u> 19. **considerable**   a) unkind   b) comfortable   c) small   d) accidental

<u>a</u> 20. **unstable**   a) steady   b) outdoors   c) cruel   d) pleasant

<u>d</u> 21. **critical**   a) rare   b) small   c) common   d) approving

<u>b</u> 22. **deliberate**   a) loud   b) accidental   c) hidden   d) late

<u>a</u> 23. **obnoxious**   a) pleasant   b) healthy   c) strong   d) pleased

<u>b</u> 24. **intentional**   a) outward   b) accidental   c) unlikely   d) unclear

<u>d</u> 25. **to linger**   a) yell   b) stay   c) remain quiet   d) rush away

SCORE: (Number correct) _____ x 4 = _____ %

Enter your score above and in the vocabulary performance chart on the inside back cover of the book.

Unit Five

Previewing the Words

Find out how many of the five words in this chapter you already know. Try to complete each sentence with the most suitable word from the list below. Use each word once.

Leave a sentence blank rather than guessing at an answer. Your purpose here is just to get a sense of the five words and what you may know about them.

betray	**comparison**	**dispute**
inhabit	**neutral**	

1. My _____*dispute*_____ with my brother over who would get the last piece of pie was settled when our father ate it.

2. About 248 million people _____*inhabit*_____ the United States of America.

3. A _____*comparison*_____ of our backgrounds and interests revealed we had a lot in common.

4. Sheila would never _____*betray*_____ you by going out with your boyfriend.

5. My mother remained _____*neutral*_____ during the quarrel between my sister and I. She said we should work it out ourselves.

Now check your answers by turning to page 147. Fix any mistakes and fill in any blank spaces by writing in the correct answers. By doing so, you will complete this introduction to the five words.

You're now ready to strengthen your knowledge of the words you already know and to master the words you're only half sure of, or don't know at all. Turn to the next page.

Five Words in Context

Figure out the meanings of the following five words by looking *closely and carefully* at the sentences below. Doing so will prepare you for the matching test and practices that follow.

1 **betray**
(bi-trā')
-*verb*

   a. Despite threats of torture, the prisoners would not **betray** their country.

   b. My brother thinks I **betrayed** him by telling our parents he was taking drugs, but I think I was helping him.

2 **comparison**
(kəm-par'-i-sən)
-*noun*

   a. A **comparison** between the cars in my price range will help me decide which one to buy.

   b. There's no **comparison** between Marty's first and second wives. His first wife was mean, but his second is very kind.

3 **dispute**
(di spyōōt')
-*noun*

   a. Business was so slow that the store's salespeople were having **disputes** over who would get the next customer.

   b. The **dispute** between the mayor and the city council is over how much money should be spent on the subways. The mayor argues for a <u>reduction</u> in spending, while the council wants an increase.

4 **inhabit**
(in-hab'-it)
-*verb*

   a. Most birds **inhabit** nests in trees, but the killdeer lives in a nest built on the ground.

   b. Although a few people have reached the North Pole, no one **inhabits** that area, except, perhaps, for Santa Claus.

5 **neutral**
(nōō'-trəl)
-*adjective*

   a. The Bradleys' marriage counselor refuses to take sides in their fights. She says that to be helpful to both of them, she must remain **neutral**.

   b. Switzerland has been a **neutral** country since 1648. Because it doesn't takes sides in other countries' wars, a <u>considerable</u> number of people have found safety there.

Matching Words and Definitions

Check your understanding of the five words by matching each word with its definition. The sentences above will help you decide on the meaning of each word.

_d_	1. **betray**	a.	an argument; quarrel
_c_	2. **comparison**	b.	not taking sides in a quarrel or war
_a_	3. **dispute**	c.	the act of checking how two or more things are alike or different; a similarity
_e_	4. **inhabit**	d.	to be disloyal to
_b_	5. **neutral**	e.	to live in

➤ Check 1

Complete each sentence below with the correct word from the box. Use each word once.

betray	comparison	dispute
inhabit	neutral	

1. The people who _____*inhabit*_____ Canada are Canadians.
2. There's more than one way to _____*betray*_____ people. You can help their enemies, or you can be disloyal in another way.
3. If you wish to remain _____*neutral*_____ in a quarrel, you cannot help either side.
4. When we say two people had a _____*dispute*_____ , we mean they had a fight of words, not a physical fight.
5. Two meanings of "_____*comparison*_____" are "the act of examining things to see how they are alike or different" (as in comparing two cars) and "a similarity" (as in the statement that there is no similiarity between Marty's two wives.)

Now check your answers to these questions by turning to page 147. Going over the answers carefully will help you prepare for the next three practices, for which answers are not given.

➤ Check 2

Complete each sentence below with the correct word from the box. Use each word once.

betray	comparison	dispute
inhabit	neutral	

1. A _____*comparison*_____ of two television sets at the store proved that the picture and color were much better on one model.
2. Steve and Rene's _____*dispute*_____ was about whose turn it was to mow the grass.
3. Bats often _____*inhabit*_____ the attics of houses, barns, and other buildings.
4. Although Elise's friends quarrcl a lot, she manages to stay _____*neutral*_____ and remain on good terms with everyone.
5. I feel that my old roommate has _____*betray*_____(e)d me. He promised to sell our stereo and split the money with me, but he left town without giving me a <u>solitary</u> cent.

➤Check 3

Circle the letter of the best answer to each question.

1. Squirrels *inhabit*   a. nuts   (b.) trees   c. their tails
2. A person *betrays* his country by   a. voting   (b.) selling its secrets
c. running for Congress
3. In baseball, the *neutral* person should be   a. the pitcher   b. the coach   (c.) the umpire
4. *Comparisons* can be helpful when you   (a.) shop   b. snore   c. shake hands
5. During a *dispute*, people always   a. wonder   (b.) disagree   c. plan

➤*Final Check:* Peace at Last

Read the following passage carefully. Then fill in each blank with a different word from the box. (Context clues will help you figure out which word goes in which blank.)

betray	comparison	dispute
inhabit	neutral	

My new apartment is so nice and quiet in (1)_____*comparison*_____ with my last one. In my old building, the people who (2)_____*inhabit*_____(e)d the apartments on both sides of me were always having (3)_____*dispute*_____s. The woman in 401 and the man in 403 would argue all the time. For example, she would yell that she had trusted him to keep her secrets, but that he had (4)_____*betray*_____(e)d her by telling everyone in the building. He would loudly insist that she was the one with the big mouth. In addition, his wife would scream at the woman for flirting with her husband. Although they tried to get me to take sides, I remained completely (5)_____*neutral*_____. I don't know who was right or wrong. I just know the frequency of their noisy arguments was too much for me, and I'm glad to be out of there.

SCORES: **Check 2** _____ %   **Check 3** _____ %   **Final Check** _____ %

Enter your scores above and in the vocabulary performance chart on the inside back cover of the book.

Previewing the Words

Find out how many of the five words in this chapter you already know. Try to complete each sentence with the most suitable word from the list below. Use each word once.

Leave a sentence blank rather than guessing at an answer. Your purpose here is just to get a sense of the five words and what you may know about them.

apparent	**automatic**	**fulfill**
influence	**transfer**	

1. My boss plans to _____*transfer*_____ me from the shipping department to receiving.

2. Ana _____*fulfill*_____(e)d her <u>ultimate</u> childhood dream when she became a professional jockey.

3. The store's _____*automatic*_____ door is broken, so you'll have to push it open yourself.

4. I was embarrassed when it became _____*apparent*_____ that I was sitting in the wrong seat.

5. My grandfather _____*influence*_____(e)d me to become a teacher. He was a teacher, and I admired him.

Now check your answers by turning to page 147. Fix any mistakes and fill in any blank spaces by writing in the correct answers. By doing so, you will complete this introduction to the five words.

You're now ready to strengthen your knowledge of the words you already know and to master the words you're only half sure of, or don't know at all. Turn to the next page.

Five Words in Context

Figure out the meanings of the following five words by looking *closely and carefully* at the sentences below. Doing so will prepare you for the matching test and practices that follow.

1 **apparent**
(ə-par'-ənt)
-*adjective*

a. Marcie's smile made it **apparent** that she did well on the test.

b. It's **apparent** that Leon and Bess have patched up their differences since they are dating steadily again.

2 **automatic**
(ô'-tə-mat'-ik)
-*adjective*

a. Our new coffee maker has an **automatic** turn-on switch. We set it at night, and it goes on by itself in the morning.

b. When you see something come rapidly toward your face, your **automatic** reaction is to blink and pull away.

3 **fulfill**
(fool-fil')
-*verb*

a. One day, Ling hopes to **fulfill** her dream of visiting China again and renewing ties with her family there.

b. Jill doesn't like her job, but she promised to stay with it at least a year, and she plans to **fulfill** that promise.

4 **influence**
(in'-floo-əns)
-*verb*

a. My father dislikes my friends because he believes they **influence** me to study less and party more.

b. The seasons **influence** my choice of activities. My preference is for indoor sports when it's cold outside.

5 **transfer**
(trans-fûr')
-*verb*

a. Before I can paint the bookcase, I have to **transfer** all the books into boxes.

b. In April, Harley was **transferred** from an army base in South Carolina to one in Virginia.

Matching Words and Definitions

Check your understanding of the five words by matching each word with its definition. The sentences above will help you decide on the meaning of each word.

_d_	1. **apparent**	a. to carry out; achieve; do
_e_	2. **automatic**	b. to move or send from one place to another
_a_	3. **fulfill**	c. to persuade someone to do something; to have an effect on
_c_	4. **influence**	d. obvious; easy to see
_b_	5. **transfer**	e. self-moving; self-acting; happening by itself without thought

➤ *Check 1*

Complete each sentence below with the correct word from the box. Use each word once.

apparent	**automatic**	**fulfill**
influence	**transfer**	

1. An _____*automatic*_____ reaction is one that you do without thinking.
2. Radio and television ads try to _____*influence*_____ people to buy certain products.
3. Because she was smiling, it was _____*apparent*_____ that she was happy about something.
4. My boss intends to assign me to another office. In other words, he wants to _____*transfer*_____ me there.
5. When you make an agreement with people, they expect you to _____*fulfill*_____ your part of the deal.

   Now check your answers to these questions by turning to page 147. Going over the answers carefully will help you prepare for the next three practices, for which answers are not given.

➤ *Check 2*

Complete each sentence below with the correct word from the box. Use each word once.

apparent	**automatic**	**fulfill**
influence	**transfer**	

1. Could you help me _____*transfer*_____ these boxes to the basement?
2. Can't you _____*influence*_____ Bobbie to find a more <u>wholesome</u> hobby than drag-racing?
3. When Sue broke her ankle, she knew her dream to win the ice-skating contest would not be _____*fulfill*_____(e)d this year.
4. Many companies have stopped giving _____*automatic*_____ pay raises to all their workers. Now, each worker must have a good work record to earn a raise.
5. It was _____*apparent*_____ that Sally was not <u>neutral</u> in the fight between her brother and sister. She bit her brother and cried, "You leave her alone!"

➤ *Check 3*

Circle the letter of the best answer to each question.

1. An *apparent* reason is **not** (a.)hidden   b. clear   c. thoughtless
2. Builders should *fulfill* (a.)their side of a contract   b. a container c. a hammer
3. To *influence* can mean the same as to a. meet   (b.)affect   c. send
4. An *automatic* machine is supposed to work a. silently   (b.)on its own c. indoors
5. If you get a job *transfer*, you might have to a. find work b. retire   (c.)move

➤ *Final Check:* A Campaign to Become Class President

Read the following passage carefully. Then fill in each blank with a different word from the box. (Context clues will help you figure out which word goes in which blank.)

apparent	automatic	fulfill
influence	transfer	

   In her senior year, Holly really wanted to be elected class president. But she knew there was no comparison between her and the other girl running for the office: the other girl was much better known and had more experience in student government. So Holly began to do all she could to (1)_____ *influence* _____ her classmates to vote for her. She found herself promising them anything they asked for. "If I'm elected," she told one, "early dismissal will be (2)_____ *automatic* _____ any time you get an A on a test." To another, she said that a hot tub would be installed in the school gym. She promised a third student that he could (3)_____ *transfer* _____ to the school across town that his girlfriend attended. As the election drew near, it became (4)_____ *apparent* _____ that Holly had a good chance of winning. This scared her because she realized that she could not (5)_____ *fulfill* _____ all her promises. Finally, she withdrew from the race, saying she couldn't keep up her grades and serve as class president too. She felt foolish for having let her desire to win run away with her good sense.

Enter your scores above and in the vocabulary performance chart on the inside back cover of the book.

Previewing the Words

Find out how many of the five words in this chapter you already know. Try to complete each sentence with the most suitable word from the list below. Use each word once.

Leave a sentence blank rather than guessing at an answer. Your purpose here is just to get a sense of the five words and what you may know about them.

accustomed	**misinterpret**	**occur**
revise	**version**	

1. Leo's headaches _____*occur*_____ after he eats certain foods.

2. It's difficult to become _____*accustomed*_____ to working the midnight shift.

3. The police officer took notes while Michael gave his _____*version*_____ of the accident.

4. I thought I had finished my essay, but when I read it the next day, I decided to _____*revise*_____ it one more time.

5. It's easy to _____*misinterpret*_____ the customs of another culture. For example, a North American may be insulted when Latin Americans intentionally arrive late to a dinner party, but the Latin Americans are doing what is considered normal in their own society.

Now check your answers by turning to page 147. Fix any mistakes and fill in any blank spaces by writing in the correct answers. By doing so, you will complete this introduction to the five words.

You're now ready to strengthen your knowledge of the words you already know and to master the words you're only half sure of, or don't know at all. Turn to the next page.

Five Words in Context

Figure out the meanings of the following five words by looking *closely and carefully* at the sentences below. Doing so will prepare you for the matching test and practices that follow.

1 **accustomed**
(ə-kus'-təmd)
-adjective

a. Although my grandfather was **accustomed** to sucking a sugar cube while he drank tea, the sugar never seemed to harm his teeth.

b. After years of <u>inhabiting</u> sunny Puerto Rico, Alma had trouble becoming **accustomed** to the snowy Minnesota weather.

2 **misinterpret**
(mis'-in-tûr'-prit)
-verb

a. When I invited my new neighbor to dinner, she **misinterpreted** my neighborliness to be romantic interest.

b. It's <u>apparent</u> that Jay **misinterpreted** his wife's request. He brought her flowers for a vase instead of flour for a cake.

3 **occur**
(ə-kûr')
-verb

a. Fights in our family **occur** rarely, but when they do take place, they are long and noisy.

b. The first moonwalk **occurred** on July 20th, 1969, after Neil Armstrong stepped on the moon and said, "That's one small step for a man, one giant leap for mankind."

4 **revise**
(ri-vīz')
-verb

a. Don't just write a paper out once and hand it in. It's important to **revise** what you write until it's in good shape.

b. Recent price increases for lumber have made it necessary for carpenters to **revise** their construction charges.

5 **version**
(vûr'-zhən)
-noun

a. Two people can see exactly the same event and still come up with two different **versions** of what happened.

b. A mystery movie produced a few years ago came out in two **versions**, each with a different ending.

Matching Words and Definitions

Check your understanding of the five words by matching each word with its definition. The sentences above will help you decide on the meaning of each word.

e	1. **accustomed (to)**	a. a report based on one point of view; a particular form of something
d	2. **misinterpret**	b. to happen; take place
b	3. **occur**	c. to change in order to improve
c	4. **revise**	d. to understand (something) incorrectly
a	5. **version**	e. in the habit of; used to something

➤ *Check 1*

Complete each sentence below with the correct word from the box. Use each word once.

accustomed	misinterpret	occur
revise	version	

1. Since my headaches _____*occur*_____ when I eat, I must be allergic to some food.

2. For someone brought up in a warm climate, it may take time to become _____*accustomed*_____ to cold weather.

3. Another word for "misunderstand" is "_____*misinterpret*_____."

4. Two meanings of "_____*version*_____" are "a report according to one source" (as an account by one eyewitness) and "a form of something" (as the movie form of a book).

5. Two meanings of "_____*revise*_____" are "to carefully read and rewrite to improve" (as with a school paper) and "to change something in order to improve or update it" (as in changing a company's prices.)

Now check your answers to these questions by turning to page 147. Going over the answers carefully will help you prepare for the next three practices, for which answers are not given.

➤ *Check 2*

Complete each sentence below with the correct word from the box. Use each word once.

accustomed	misinterpret	occur
revise	version	

1. Dad helped me to _____*revise*_____ the speech I'm giving in class tomorrow.

2. Although Kate claims that Luz started the fight, Luz's _____*version*_____ of what happened is quite different.

3. My boss said, "Don't _____*misinterpret*_____ my <u>critical</u> remarks to mean I don't like you. I do like you and want to help you improve your work."

4. It took Pauline a few visits to her boyfriend Robert's house to become _____*accustomed*_____ to hearing everyone call him "Bobby."

5. The people in the fishing boat couldn't believe a storm could _____*occur*_____ with so little warning. One minute the sun was out, and the next minute it was pouring.

➤ *Check 3*

A. Circle **C** if the italicized word is used **correctly**. Circle **I** if the word is used **incorrectly**.

C Ⓘ 1. My mother is so *accustomed* to cigarettes that she can't stand to be in the same room with smoke.

Ⓒ I 2. Juries often have to decide whose *version* of events to believe.

Ⓒ I 3. When editors *revise* dictionaries, they add new words and new meanings for old words.

C Ⓘ 4. I like to *occur* at the office after everyone else has left so that I can do some work in quiet.

B.   5. In *misinterpret,* the prefix *mis-* means "wrongly." Thus *misinterpret* means "to interpret (make sense of) wrongly." In the blanks, write two more words beginning with *mis-* that include the meaning "wrongly." (If you wish, get help from the dictionary.)

      <u>   *Answers will vary.*   </u>   _____

➤ *Final Check:* **A French Boss**

Read the following passage carefully. Then fill in each blank with a different word from the box. (Context clues will help you figure out which word goes in which blank.)

accustomed	misinterpret	occur
revise	version	

When I first started working for my boss, I could hardly understand a word she said. She's French, and it took me quite a while before I was (1)_____*accustomed*_____ to her accent. For the first few weeks, whenever she told me to type something, I would (2)_____*misinterpret*_____ what she said. I'd type what I thought she said and bring it to her. She would say it wasn't right, and then I'd have to (3)_____*revise*_____ the pages I had typed. Now mistakes like that hardly ever (4)_____*occur*_____. I am able to understand her much better, and my (5)_____*version*_____ of a letter is nearly always the same as hers.

SCORES: **Check 2** _____ %	**Check 3** _____ %	**Final Check** _____ %

Enter your scores above and in the vocabulary performance chart on the inside back cover of the book.

28

Previewing the Words

Find out how many of the five words in this chapter you already know. Try to complete each sentence with the most suitable word from the list below. Use each word once.

Leave a sentence blank rather than guessing at an answer. Your purpose here is just to get a sense of the five words and what you may know about them.

brutal	**discipline**	**eliminate**
furthermore	**resort**	

1. Our tap water looks rusty. _____*Furthermore*_____, it tastes like medicine.

2. The people celebrated the downfall of their _____*brutal*_____ king.

3. Normal shampoo won't _____*eliminate*_____ head lice. To kill all the lice and their eggs, you must use a special medication.

4. Mr. Fine was <u>accustomed</u> to mowing his own grass, but after he broke his hip, he had to _____*resort*_____ to a lawn service.

5. The ballplayer was put out of the game for hitting an umpire. The player was also _____*discipline*_____(e)d with a $2,000 fine.

Now check your answers by turning to page 147. Fix any mistakes and fill in any blank spaces by writing in the correct answers. By doing so, you will complete this introduction to the five words.

You're now ready to strengthen your knowledge of the words you already know and to master the words you're only half sure of, or don't know at all. Turn to the next page.

Five Words in Context

Figure out the meanings of the following five words by looking *closely and carefully* at the sentences below. Doing so will prepare you for the matching test and practices that follow.

1 **brutal**
(broot'-l)
-*adjective*

  a. Brenda's first husband was **brutal**. When he beat her for the third time, she finally left him.

  b. Ed's mother never hit him, but she was **brutal**. Her cruel words were more painful than any beating could have been.

2 **discipline**
(dis'-ə-plin)
-*verb*

  a. I wish my neighbor would **discipline** his dog not to utilize our garbage cans as a snack bar.

  b. Jose wants to influence his children to be nonviolent, so he **disciplines** them in gentle ways, such as sending them to their rooms for some quiet "time out."

3 **eliminate**
(i-lim'-ə-nāt')
-*verb*

  a. If you hang clothes up right after the dryer stops, you can **eliminate** the need to iron many items.

  b. A speech therapist helped my cousin totally **eliminate** his stutter by the time he went to high school.

4 **furthermore**
(fûr'-thər-môr')
-*adverb*

  a. "I don't believe your story about a flat tire," said Herb's boss, "and **furthermore**, I haven't believed any of your other excuses for being late."

  b. The Hawks will win because they are a talented team. **Furthermore**, they are coached well.

5 **resort**
(ri-zôrt')
-*verb*

  a. Once Bernie was so low on money that he **resorted** to selling his blood to a blood bank.

  b. I prefer to exercise by bicycling outdoors. But when the weather is bad, I **resort** to my exercise bike.

Matching Words and Definitions

Check your understanding of the five words by matching each word with its definition. The sentences above will help you decide on the meaning of each word.

_e_	1. **brutal**	a.	to train through instruction and practice; to punish
_a_	2. **discipline**	b.	to turn or go (to) for help; make use of
_d_	3. **eliminate**	c.	in addition; besides
_c_	4. **furthermore**	d.	to get rid of
_b_	5. **resort (to)**	e.	cruel; heartless

➤ *Check 1*

Complete each sentence below with the correct word from the box. Use each word once.

brutal	discipline	eliminate
furthermore	resort	

1. People take aspirin to _____*eliminate*_____ headaches.

2. Someone without mercy can be _____*brutal*_____.

3. If you were low on cash, would you _____*resort*_____ to selling your blood?

4. Another way of saying "in addition" is "_____*furthermore*_____."

5. Two meanings of "_____*discipline*_____" are "to train" and "to punish."

Now check your answers to these questions by turning to page 147. Going over the answers carefully will help you prepare for the next three practices, for which answers are not given.

➤ *Check 2*

Complete each sentence below with the correct word from the box. Use each word once.

brutal	discipline	eliminate
furthermore	resort	

1. Tamar is an outstanding student; _____*furthermore*_____, she's an excellent drummer.

2. Because my father has high blood pressure, he's supposed to avoid <u>stress</u> and _____*eliminate*_____ salt from his diet.

3. Our puppy is so anxious to please us that we can _____*discipline*_____ her for wetting the floor simply by scolding.

4. When our car ran out of gas and we had no money, we had to _____*resort*_____ to walking all the way home.

5. Most veal is the result of _____*brutal*_____ treatment of baby calves, who are forced to spend all of their short lives in dark pens too small to lie down in.

➤ *Check 3*

Circle the letter of the best answer to each question.

1. The **opposite** of *brutal* is   a. attractive   (b.) kind   c. honest

2. The **opposite** of *eliminate* is: a. remove   b. weigh   (c.) add

3. To *discipline* can mean the **same** as to   (a.) teach   b. know   c. learn

4. *Furthermore* means the **same** as   a. after   b. instead of   (c.) also

5. We are more likely to *resort* to something   a. harmful   b. untrained   (c.) useful

➤ *Final Check:* Teaching a Lesson

Read the following passage carefully. Then fill in each blank with a different word from the box. (Context clues will help you figure out which word goes in which blank.)

brutal	discipline	eliminate
furthermore	resort	

One reason that parents (1)_____*discipline*_____ children is in order to (2)_____*eliminate*_____ behaviors that are rude or hurtful. Unfortunately, some parents use (3)_____*brutal*_____ punishments to teach their children to be good. But cruel treatment only teaches children that it's okay for them to (4)_____*resort*_____ to hitting and punching when they need to solve a problem. (5)_____*Furthermore*_____, children who are hit too often and too hard are deprived of a feeling of security. They grow up anticipating that the whole world will be cruel to them and thus often become cruel to others.

SCORES:	Check 2 _____ %	Check 3 _____ %	Final Check _____ %

Enter your scores above and in the vocabulary performance chart on the inside back cover of the book.

Previewing the Words

Find out how many of the five words in this chapter you already know. Try to complete each sentence with the most suitable word from the list below. Use each word once.

Leave a sentence blank rather than guessing at an answer. Your purpose here is just to get a sense of the five words and what you may know about them.

attitude	contrast	excessive
fragile	indicate	

1. Randy came to the party with a poor _____*attitude*_____, convinced that he would have a lousy time.

2. My sister's tiny build makes her look _____*fragile*_____, but she is really as strong as an ox.

3. Some people say a red sunset _____*indicate*_____s that the weather will be fair the next day.

4. Jodi is worried that Wayne's interest in gambling, which used to be minor, is becoming _____*excessive*_____.

5. I visited the Greenes' house when they first moved in and again six months later, and the _____*contrast*_____ in the house was amazing. They'd <u>eliminated</u> the ugly dark features of the house and turned it into a lovely, cheerful place.

Now check your answers by turning to page 147. Fix any mistakes and fill in any blank spaces by writing in the correct answers. By doing so, you will complete this introduction to the five words.

You're now ready to strengthen your knowledge of the words you already know and to master the words you're only half sure of, or don't know at all. Turn to the next page.

Five Words in Context

Figure out the meanings of the following five words by looking *closely and carefully* at the sentences below. Doing so will prepare you for the matching test and practices that follow.

1 **attitude**
(at'-i-tōōd')
-noun

   a. The doctor believes that Art's good **attitude** helped him to recover from his serious illness.

   b. Athletes have to <u>discipline</u> themselves not to let a loss affect their **attitude** at their next game.

2 **contrast**
(kən'-trast')
-noun

   a. I was struck by the **contrast** between the fancy cars and houses north of Main Street and the very poor neighborhood to the south.

   b. Peggy is very independent from her parents. In **contrast**, her brother Reggie, overly <u>dependent</u>, is always asking them for money.

3 **excessive**
(ik-ses'-iv)
-adjective

   a. **Excessive** speed caused the accident.

   b. Everyone is concerned about their children's health, but Mrs. Hill's worry is **excessive**. She <u>automatically</u> rushes her little boy to the doctor even when he has the slightest problem.

4 **fragile**
(fraj'-əl)
-adjective

   a. The lamp is **fragile**, so be careful when you pack it.

   b. When our children were little, we put anything **fragile** at least five feet from the ground, where it couldn't be broken by curious fingers.

5 **indicate**
(in'-də-kāt')
-verb

   a. Jeff's frown seemed to **indicate** that he's unhappy with our plan.

   b. The parking lot worker waved to **indicate** that we should pull all the way up to the fence.

Matching Words and Definitions

Check your understanding of the five words by matching each word with its definition. The sentences above will help you decide on the meaning of each word.

_c_	1. **attitude**	a. too much; more than usual or proper
_e_	2. **contrast**	b. easily damaged or broken
_a_	3. **excessive**	c. frame of mind; mood; feeling
_b_	4. **fragile**	d. to be a sign; to point out
_d_	5. **indicate**	e. a striking difference; a comparison made to show differences

➤Check 1

Complete each sentence below with the correct word from the box. Use each word once.

attitude	contrast	excessive
fragile	indicate	

1. Ben's holiday eating was _____*excessive*_____. In other words, he ate too much.

2. After losing three basketball games in a row, the players had a poor

   _____*attitude*_____.

3. Something _____*fragile*_____ can be damaged easily.

4. Two meanings of "_____*indicate*_____" are "to serve as a sign" (as a frown is a sign of unhappiness) and "to show" (as an arrow shows the way).

5. Two meanings of "_____*contrast*_____" are "a lack of similarity between two things" and "an examination done in order to see differences."

Now check your answers to these questions by turning to page 147. Going over the answers carefully will help you prepare for the next three practices, for which answers are not given.

➤Check 2

Complete each sentence below with the correct word from the box. Use each word once.

attitude	contrast	excessive
fragile	indicate	

1. _____*Excessive*_____ praise can be as hard for a child to cope with as not enough praise.

2. I learned the hard way that the small red light on the dashboard _____*indicate*_____s that the car is low on oil.

3. On the package Juanita mailed, she wrote, "_____*Fragile*_____—HANDLE WITH CARE!" But when her dishes arrived, they were broken anyway.

4. There can be a great _____*contrast*_____ in the weather in spring. One day can be warm and sunny, and the next cold and gloomy.

5. Doug's _____*attitude*_____ toward school is poor. He's almost always absent or late for class. Furthermore, he rarely does the homework.

➤ Check 3

Circle the letter of the best answer to each question.

1. "A good *attitude*" means the same as a good   a. deed   ⓑ state of mind   c. friendship
2. The biggest *contrast* is between day and   ⓐ night   b. morning   c. noon
3. An example of something *fragile* is a   a. rock   b. tennis shoe   ⓒ wine glass
4. An *excessive* amount of ice cream might be enough for   a. a taste   b. a cone
   ⓒ a stomach ache
5. When ordering a pizza, you must *indicate* the   a. date   ⓑ kind of topping   c. tax

➤ Final Check: A House Versus a Home

Here is a final opportunity for you to strengthen your knowledge of the five words. First read the following passage carefully. Then fill in each blank with a word from the box (Context clues will help you figure out which word goes in which blank.) Use each word once.

attitude	contrast	excessive
fragile	indicate	

The Randolph sisters, Sadie and Esther, live just a block away from each other. Sadie constantly complains that the people in town are cold and unfriendly, while Esther finds them warm and pleasant.

Although Sadie can't see it, the difference is in the way they approach those people. Sadie and her husband have a lovely house. It's filled with beautiful antique furniture and glassware that is so (1)_____*fragile*_____ it could easily be broken by a careless guest or adventurous child. Whenever someone is visiting, Sadie and her husband are constantly "straightening up." Their behavior seems to (2)_____*indicate*_____ that they put more of an emphasis on the looks of their house than on the comfort of their guests. As a result, their nervous guests behave with (3)_____*excessive*_____ care—and they leave as soon as possible.

In (4)_____*contrast*_____, Esther's house is not fancy at all. In fact, it's almost shabby. But she and her husband have a relaxed, friendly (5)_____*attitude*_____ toward visitors, who don't have to worry about an accident occurring with an expensive piece of furniture or vase. Esther's house is a place where people can drop in, put their feet up on the coffee table, and feel at home.

SCORES:	Check 2 ____ %		Check 3 ____ %		Final Check ____ %

Enter your scores above and in the vocabulary performance chart on the inside back cover of the book.

Previewing the Words

Find out how many of the five words in this chapter you already know. Try to complete each sentence with the most suitable word from the list below. Use each word once.

Leave a sentence blank rather than guessing at an answer. Your purpose here is just to get a sense of the five words and what you may know about them.

adequate	**awkward**	**customary**
respond	**vanish**	

1. Theo outgrew his _____*awkward*_____ stage and became an excellent athlete.

2. On our camping trip, I enjoyed hearing the loons _____*respond*_____ to one another's calls across the lake.

3. Chun's apartment is small, but it's _____*adequate*_____ for her needs.

4. The new manager was surprised to learn it was _____*customary*_____ in this company for employees to have Columbus Day off.

5. My brother and I used to argue a lot, but as soon as a <u>dispute</u> ended, our bad feelings _____*vanish*_____(e)d and we were best of friends again.

Now check your answers by turning to page 147. Fix any mistakes and fill in any blank spaces by writing in the correct answers. By doing so, you will complete this introduction to the five words.

You're now ready to strengthen your knowledge of the words you already know and to master the words you're only half sure of, or don't know at all. Turn to the next page.

Five Words in Context

Figure out the meanings of the following five words by looking *closely and carefully* at the sentences below. Doing so will prepare you for the matching test and practices that follow.

1 **adequate**
(ad'-ə-kwit)
-adjective

    a. When I didn't have time to wash the windows, I had to <u>resort</u> to hiring a neighbor's child to do it. He did an **adequate** job; not perfect, but good enough.

    b. Open sandals are not **adequate** footwear for factory work. You should wear heavy shoes to protect your feet.

2 **awkward**
(ôk'-wərd)
-adjective

    a. When I was 13, I was very **awkward**. My feet seemed too big, and I was always tripping over things.

    b. It was **awkward** when the teacher asked Dee a very personal question in front of the entire class.

3 **customary**
(kus'-tə-mer'-ē)
-adjective

    a. In some towns, it's **customary** for the "Welcome Wagon" to visit newcomers and tell them about the town.

    b. When offered a meal in Japan, it's **customary** to insist one is not hungry and to accept the food only after it's been offered several times.

4 **respond**
(ri-spond')
-verb

    a. I will not **respond** to such a rude question.

    b. The group of men whistled and called out to Kim as she walked by, but she didn't **respond** at all. She simply kept walking.

5 **vanish**
(van'-ish)
-verb

    a. The magician made the rabbit **vanish** by slipping it under a secret door.

    b. The happy mood at our party **vanished** when we heard that our guest of honor had been <u>brutally</u> beaten on his way to our house.

Matching Words and Definitions

Check your understanding of the five words by matching each word with its definition. The sentences above will help you decide on the meaning of each word.

_c_	1. **adequate**	a. clumsy; embarrassing
_a_	2. **awkward**	b. to answer; to act in return
_d_	3. **customary**	c. good enough (to meet the need); satisfactory
_b_	4. **respond**	d. usual; commonly done
_e_	5. **vanish**	e. to disappear from sight; to come to an end

➤Check 1

Complete each sentence below with the correct word from the box. Use each word once.

adequate	awkward	customary
respond	vanish	

1. People's habits can be referred to as their _____*customary*_____ behavior.
2. I'd love a huge apartment, but this small one is _____*adequate*_____—it serves my needs.
3. When asked a question, we usually _____*respond*_____, even if it's only to say, "I don't know."
4. Two meanings of "_____*vanish*_____" are "to stop being seen, but still exist" and "to stop existing."
5. Two meanings of "_____*awkward*_____" are "ungraceful" and "embarrassing."

Now check your answers to these questions by turning to page 147. Going over the answers carefully will help you prepare for the next three practices, for which answers are not given.

➤Check 2

Complete each sentence below with the correct word from the box. Use each word once.

adequate	awkward	customary
respond	vanish	

1. A cold will _____*vanish*_____ after a week or so whether you treat it or not.
2. Nick's old car may not be attractive, but it's _____*adequate*_____ for getting him around town.
3. I often find it _____*awkward*_____ to ask a girl for a date. Now that girls are asking guys for dates, they see how embarrassing it can be.
4. When Clarita arrived at her grandmother's house for their weekly outing, she became concerned when the older woman did not _____*respond*_____ to the doorbell.
5. Americans usually eat their big meal in the evening. In Ireland, however, it is _____*customary*_____ to eat a big dinner in the afternoon and a light meal at night.

➤ *Check 3*

Circle the letter of the best answer to each question.

1. "An *adequate* grade" probably means   a. an A   ⓑ a C   c. an F
2. An *awkward* situation would be   a. illegal   b. hidden   ⓒ uncomfortable
3. A *customary* greeting is   a. old-fashioned   ⓑ "hello"   c. embarrassing
4. Something that *vanishes* cannot be   ⓐ seen   b. imagined   c. real
5. You usually have to *respond* to   ⓐ an invitation   b. a sign   c. a TV program

➤ *Final Check:* **Kevin's First Date**

Here is a final opportunity for you to strengthen your knowledge of the five words. First read the following passage carefully. Then fill in each blank with a word from the box. (Context clues will help you figure out which word goes in which blank.) Use each word once.

adequate	awkward	customary
respond	vanish	

   If you ask Kevin what the most (1)_____*awkward*_____ time of his life was, he will surely tell you about his first date, to the ninth-grade dance. Between the time he rang the girl's doorbell and the time the girl's father answered, he forgot his date's name. Completely. He mumbled something about school (he did remember the school's name), and the girl's father let him in. The man then shot some questions at Kevin, to make sure he was a(n) (2)_____*adequate*_____ date for his darling daughter. Kevin could barely (3)_____*respond*_____ to the questions because his nervous, 13-year-old voice squeaked and cracked so much.

   Since it was (4)_____*customary*_____ for boys to bring flowers on this special occasion, Kevin had done so. But when his date came down the stairs in a thin-strapped pink dress and he opened the florist's box, he became even more nervous. Inside was an <u>excessively</u> large flower in a bright orange color that clashed with the pink dress. He tried to pin the giant blossom onto the gown, stuck his finger, and bled—on the dress. He wanted to (5)_____*vanish*_____ from the face of the earth and never be seen again. He even considered <u>transferring</u> to another school. As it was, he developed such a poor <u>attitude</u> about dating that he didn't ask another girl out for the next two years.

SCORES:	Check 2 _____%	Check 3 _____%	Final Check _____%

Enter your scores above and in the vocabulary performance chart on the inside back cover of the book.

UNIT FIVE: Test 1

PART A
Complete each sentence with a word from the box. Use each word once.

automatic	brutal	fragile	fulfill	inhabit
neutral	occur	revise	transfer	vanish

1. Wouldn't it be wonderful if dirt _____*vanish*_____(e)d as easily and completely in real life as it does on the soap ads?

2. The boxing match was unfair because the referee wasn't really _____*neutral*_____—he had bet on the champ.

3. Ronald always shows his short stories to his wife and then _____*revise*_____s them after hearing her comments.

4. Most people who _____*inhabit*_____ a wealthy nation like ours cannot truly imagine the terrible poverty in Third World nations.

5. Many new cameras are fully _____*automatic*_____. That is, they focus, advance, and adjust for poor light all by themselves.

6. My suitcase was so heavy that I had to _____*transfer*_____ it from my right hand to my left and then back to my right hand again.

7. Some people say they know when an earthquake will _____*occur*_____, but quakes never seem to happen exactly when predicted.

8. The Sunshine Foundation _____*fulfill*_____s the wishes of children who are dying. For example, it has arranged for many children to visit Disney World or to meet their favorite athlete.

9. I think it is _____*brutal*_____ to keep chickens in crowded conditions and then cut off their beaks to keep them from pecking at each other.

10. The lacy cookies that Mrs. Nordstrom makes at Christmas are so

    _____*fragile*_____ that if you're not careful, they crumble into bits.

(Continues on next page)

PART B

Circle **C** if the italicized word is used **correctly**. Circle **I** if the word is used **incorrectly**.

C (I) 11.   "To *misinterpret* my instructions," said the teacher, "listen carefully."

(C) I 12.   Although Edward has a hot temper, I don't think he'd ever *resort* to violence.

(C) I 13.   Don't make *comparisons* between your children. Instead, look for each child's good points.

C (I) 14.   There's an interesting *contrast* between fennel seed and licorice—they taste amazingly alike.

(C) I 15.   Bill went to the police and *betrayed* the member of his gang who purposely shot a three-year-old.

(C) I 16.   When my sister was first allowed to wear makeup, she wore an *excessive* amount, but now she hardly wears any.

C (I) 17.   If you need to gain weight, you can *eliminate* more calories to your diet by adding nuts and avocado to your meals.

(C) I 18.   For some people, five hours of sleep each night may provide *adequate* rest. Others may need as many as ten hours.

C (I) 19.   It's *apparent* that Kate has willpower. For years, she's been saying she'll quit smoking, and she's smoking more than ever now.

C (I) 20.   The famous ballet dancer is so *awkward* that he's known as "The Hummingbird"—he moves as though his feet don't touch the ground.

(C) I 21.   It was *customary* for people to smile at everyone else in Jeanie's small hometown. Although she now lives in a big city, she still smiles at every stranger she passes.

(C) I 22.   When two girls said they were four hours late for school because of a flat tire, the principal sat them apart and asked each to write down her *version* of what had happened and where.

C (I) 23.   I'm so *accustomed* to living near the fire department that whenever a siren goes off, my heart beats faster and the hairs on my arms stand on end.

(C) I 24.   Just as hands point out the time on a clock, flowers *indicated* the time in "flower clocks." In these 19th-century gardens, flowers were planted which were known to open and close at certain times.

C (I) 25.   While everyone else was talking and dancing at the party, Liz and Felipe—hugging, kissing, and admiring each other—were having a romantic *dispute* in the corner.

> **SCORE:** (Number correct) _____ x 4 = _____ %

Enter your score above and in the vocabulary performance chart on the inside back cover of the book.

UNIT FIVE: Test 2

PART A: Synonyms
In the space provided, write the letter of the choice that is most nearly the **same** in meaning as the boldfaced word.

_b_ 1. **to inhabit** a) enter b) live in c) get used to d) understand

_c_ 2. **to fulfill** a) fill up b) correct c) carry out d) carry

_d_ 3. **to influence** a) avoid b) force c) please d) affect

_b_ 4. **to transfer** a) avoid b) move c) keep d) answer

_c_ 5. **to occur** a) delay b) surprise c) happen
d) happen at the same time

_c_ 6. **to revise** a) give advice b) go back c) change d) awaken

_d_ 7. **a version** a) rhyme b) dislike c) reason d) form

_a_ 8. **to discipline** a) train b) harm c) remove d) affect

_b_ 9. **furthermore** a) instead of b) also c) because d) but

_d_ 10. **to resort to** a) vacation at b) sort c) wonder about
d) make use of

_a_ 11. **an attitude** a) outlook b) height c) quarrel d) rule

_d_ 12. **to indicate** a) win b) expect c) look for d) point out

_b_ 13. **to respond to** a) know b) answer c) believe d) desire

(Continues on next page)

PART B: Antonyms
In the space provided, write the letter of the choice that is most nearly the **opposite** in meaning to the boldfaced word.

_a_ 14. **apparent**   a) hidden   b) above   c) under   d) unnatural

_b_ 15. **neutral**   a) relaxed   b) taking sides   c) old   d) not enough

_b_ 16. **brutal**   a) loyal   b) kind   c) unclear   d) healthy

_d_ 17. **customary**   a) hidden   b) unfriendly   c) well-known
d) unusual

_a_ 18. **awkward**   a) graceful   b) outward   c) noisy   d) kind

_b_ 19. **a contrast**   a) being together   b) similarity   c) disagreement
d) favorite

_a_ 20. **to vanish**   a) appear   b) disappear   c) build   d) destroy

_d_ 21. **a dispute**   a) disappointment   b) friend   c) hope   d) agreement

_c_ 22. **excessive**   a) leftover   b) indoors   c) not enough   d) late

_d_ 23. **to betray**   a) leave   b) give   c) get stronger   d) be loyal

_d_ 24. **accustomed to**   a) attracted to   b) unaware of   c) aware of
d) not in the habit of

_a_ 25. **fragile**   a) tough   b) correct   c) unwrapped   d) graceful

SCORE: (Number correct) _____ x 4 = _____ %

Enter your score above and in the vocabulary performance chart on the inside back cover of the book.

A. Limited Answer Key

An Important Note: Be sure to use this answer key as a learning tool only. You should not turn to this key until you have considered carefully the sentence in which a given word appears.

Used properly, the key will help you to learn words and to prepare for the activities and tests for which answers are not given. For ease of reference, the title of the "Final Check" passage in each chapter appears in parentheses.

Chapter 1 (Children's Lies)

Previewing the Words	Check 1
1. deceive	1. communicate
2. communicate	2. deceive
3. fiction	3. theory
4. theory	4. Fiction
5. earnest	5. earnest

Chapter 2 (A Mysterious Letter)

Previewing the Words	Check 1
1. emotion	1. emotion
2. bewilder	2. bewilder
3. investigate	3. legible
4. appropriate	4. investigate
5. legible	5. appropriate

Chapter 3 (Differing Attitudes About Money)

Previewing the Words	Check 1
1. economical	1. security
2. security	2. burden
3. sympathize	3. economical
4. burden	4. extravagant
5. extravagant	5. sympathize

Chapter 4 (Fixing Up Furniture)

Previewing the Words	Check 1
1. evident	1. evident
2. determine	2. determine
3. dispose	3. restore
4. preserve	4. preserve
5. restore	5. dispose

Chapter 5 (Fear of Public Speaking)

Previewing the Words	Check 1
1. overwhelm	1. inferior
2. thorough	2. overwhelm
3. inferior	3. convince
4. anxious	4. anxious
5. convince	5. thorough

Chapter 6 (Mrs. Thornton's Condition)

Previewing the Words	Check 1
1. dramatic	1. dramatic
2. frank	2. impression
3. illustrate	3. comprehend
4. comprehend	4. frank
5. impression	5. illustrate

Chapter 7 (Traveling with Children)

Previewing the Words	Check 1
1. stress	1. unanimous
2. vary	2. vary
3. unanimous	3. stress
4. conflict	4. conflict
5. vicinity	5. vicinity

Chapter 8 (Saving Earth's Natural Supplies)

Previewing the Words	Check 1
1. renew	1. possess
2. sufficient	2. resource
3. possess	3. procedure
4. resource	4. sufficient
5. procedure	5. renew

Chapter 9 (Toasters)

Previewing the Words	Check 1
1. current	1. originate
2. maintain	2. reliable
3. minimum	3. current
4. reliable	4. minimum
5. originate	5. maintain

Chapter 10 (A Mean Man)

Previewing the Words	Check 1
1. objection	1. penalize
2. hesitate	2. advise
3. advise	3. deprive
4. deprive	4. hesitate
5. penalize	5. objection

Chapter 11 (Coming Out of a Coma)

Previewing the Words	Check 1
1. internal	1. remedy
2. incredible	2. external
3. remedy	3. internal
4. conscious	4. incredible
5. external	5. conscious

Chapter 12 (The Office Doughnut Contest)

Previewing the Words	Check 1
1. exhaust	1. objective
2. maximum	2. maximum
3. objective	3. protest
4. protest	4. assume
5. assume	5. exhaust

Chapter 13 (Barbara's Date with Her Cousin)

Previewing the Words	Check 1
1. rejection	1. rejection
2. pursue	2. scarce
3. accompany	3. accompany
4. desperate	4. desperate
5. scarce	5. pursue

Chapter 14 (Big Brothers and Sisters)

Previewing the Words	Check 1
1. appeal	1. potential
2. potential	2. establish
3. variety	3. wholesome
4. establish	4. variety
5. wholesome	5. appeal

Chapter 15 (Differences in a Gym Program)

Previewing the Words	Check 1
1. ultimate	1. ultimate
2. interpret	2. vague
3. emphasis	3. emphasis
4. vague	4. interpret
5. propose	5. propose

Chapter 16 (Don's Garden)

Previewing the Words	Check 1
1. transform	1. challenge
2. challenge	2. transform
3. surplus	3. surplus
4. fertile	4. peculiar
5. peculiar	5. fertile

Chapter 17 (Lizzie's Lies)

Previewing the Words	Check 1
1. transparent	1. counsel
2. detect	2. complicate
3. counsel	3. detect
4. complicate	4. conscience
5. conscience	5. transparent

Chapter 18 (Helpful Robots)

Previewing the Words	Check 1
1. solitary	1. suitable
2. preference	2. preference
3. dependent	3. principal
4. suitable	4. dependent
5. principal	5. solitary

Chapter 19 (My Annoying Kid Brother)

Previewing the Words	Check 1
1. interference	1. Interference
2. aggravate	2. cease
3. cease	3. Humane
4. humane	4. obnoxious
5. obnoxious	5. aggravate

Chapter 20 (Barry's Job Evaluation)

Previewing the Words	Check 1
1. critical	1. category
2. frustration	2. analyze
3. category	3. deliberate
4. analyze	4. critical
5. deliberate	5. frustration

Chapter 21 (The Vacuum Cleaner Salesman)

Previewing the Words	Check 1
1. reduction	1. reduction
2. distinct	2. abundant
3. abundant	3. exaggerate
4. demonstrate	4. distinct
5. exaggerate	5. demonstrate

Chapter 22 ("Meet You at the Park!")

Previewing the Words	Check 1
1. anticipate	1. linger
2. miserable	2. specific
3. reluctant	3. reluctant
4. linger	4. anticipate
5. specific	5. miserable

Chapter 23 (An Unhappy Playboy)

Previewing the Words	*Check 1*
1. represent	1. triumph
2. artificial	2. temporary
3. triumph	3. Artificial
4. frequency	4. frequency
5. temporary	5. represent

Chapter 24 (A Bad Taste Party)

Previewing the Words	*Check 1*
1. unstable	1. coincide
2. considerable	2. considerable
3. coincide	3. intentional
4. utilize	4. utilize
5. intentional	5. unstable

Chapter 25 (Peace at Last)

Previewing the Words	*Check 1*
1. dispute	1. inhabit
2. inhabit	2. betray
3. comparison	3. neutral
4. betray	4. dispute
5. neutral	5. comparison

Chapter 26 (A Campaign to Become Class President)

Previewing the Words	*Check 1*
1. transfer	1. automatic
2. fulfill	2. influence
3. automatic	3. apparent
4. apparent	4. transfer
5. influence	5. fulfill

Chapter 27 (A French Boss)

Previewing the Words	*Check 1*
1. occur	1. occur
2. accustomed	2. accustomed
3. version	3. misinterpret
4. revise	4. version
5. misinterpret	5. revise

Chapter 28 (Teaching a Lesson)

Previewing the Words	*Check 1*
1. Furthermore	1. eliminate
2. brutal	2. brutal
3. eliminate	3. resort
4. resort	4. furthermore
5. discipline	5. discipline

Chapter 29 (A House Versus a Home)

Previewing the Words	*Check 1*
1. attitude	1. excessive
2. fragile	2. attitude
3. indicate	3. fragile
4. excessive	4. indicate
5. contrast	5. contrast

Chapter 30 (Kevin's First Date)

Previewing the Words	*Check 1*
1. awkward	1. customary
2. respond	2. adequate
3. adequate	3. respond
4. customary	4. vanish
5. vanish	5. awkward

B. Dictionary Use

It isn't always possible to figure out the meaning of a word from its context, and that's where a dictionary comes in. Following is some basic information to help you use a dictionary.

HOW TO FIND A WORD

A dictionary contains so many words that it can take a while to find the one you're looking for. But if you know how to use guide words, you can find a word rather quickly. *Guide words* are the two words at the top of each dictionary page. The first guide word tells what the first word is on the page. The second guide word tells what the last word is on that page. The other words on a page fall alphabetically between the two guide words. So when you look up a word, find the two guide words that alphabetically surround the word you're looking for.

• Which of the following pair of guide words would be on a page with the word *litigate*?

   light / lily   **lodger / longhand**   ⟨ **liquid / litter** ⟩

The answer to this question and the ones that follow are given on the next page.

HOW TO USE A DICTIONARY LISTING

A dictionary listing includes many pieces of information. For example, here is a listing from the *Random House College Dictionary*, Paperback Edition. Note that it includes much more than just a definition.

> **thun•der** (thun'dər), *n.* **1.** the explosive sound following an electrical charge of lightning. **2.** any loud, resounding noise. — *v.* **3.** to give forth thunder **4.** To make a loud, resounding noise like thunder. **5.** to utter loudly or threateningly.

Key parts of a dictionary entry are listed and explained below.

1. Syllables. Dots separate dictionary entry words into syllables. Note that *thunder* has one dot, which breaks the word into two syllables.

• To practice seeing the syllable breakdown in a dictionary entry, write the number of syllables in each word below.

   out•pa•tient _3_   **Mis•sis•sip•pi** _4_   **re•frig•er•a•tor** _5_

2. Pronunciation guide. The information within parentheses after the entry word shows how to pronounce the entry word. This pronunciation guide includes two types of symbols: pronunciation symbols and accent marks.

*a. **Pronunciation symbols*** show the consonant and vowel sounds in a word. The consonant sounds are probably very familiar to you, but you may find it helpful to review some of the sounds of the vowels—*a, e, i, o,* and *u.* Every dictionary has a key explaining the sounds of its pronunciation symbols, including the long and short sounds of vowels.

Long vowels have the sound of their own names. For example, the *a* in *pay* and the *o* in *no* both have long vowel sounds. Long vowel sounds are shown by a straight line above the vowel.

In the *Random House College Dictionary,* the *short vowels* are shown by the use of the vowel itself, with no other markings. Thus the *u* in the first syllable of *thunder* is a short *u.* What do the short vowels sound like? Below are words from the *RHCD* pronunciation key which illustrate the *short vowel* sounds.

    a bat   **e** set   **i** big   **o** box   **u** up

This key means, for example, that the *a* in *bat* has the short-*a* sound

- Which of the words below has a short vowel sound? Which has a long vowel sound?

    camp _short_   **pie** _long_   **silk** _short_

Another pronunciation symbol is the *schwa,* which looks like an upside-down *e.* It stands for certain rapidly spoken, unaccented vowel sounds, such as the *a* in *above,* the *e* in *item,* the *i* in *easily,* the *o* in *gallop,* and the *u* in *circus.* Here are three words that include the schwa sound:

    in•fant (in'fənt)   **sim•ple** (sim'pəl)   **de•liv•er** (di-liv'ər)

- Which syllable in *thunder* contains the schwa sound, the first or the second? _second_

*b. **Accent marks*** are small black marks that tell you which syllable to stress, or accent, as you say a word. An accent mark follows *thun* in the pronunciation guide for *thunder,* which tells you to stress the first syllable of *thunder.* Syllables with no accent mark are not stressed. Some syllables are in between, and they are marked with a lighter accent mark.

- Which syllable has the stronger accent in *ultimatum?*

    ul•ti•mat•um (ul'tə-mā'təm) _third_

3. Parts of Speech. After the pronunciation key and before each set of definitions, the entry word's parts of speech are given. The parts of speech are abbreviated as follows:

    noun—*n.*   pronoun—*pron.*   adjective—*adj.*
    adverb—*adv.*   verb—*v.*

- The listing for *thunder* shows it has two parts of speech. Write them below:

    noun   _verb_

4. Definitions. Words often have more than one meaning. When they do, each meaning is usually numbered in the dictionary. You can tell which definition of a word fits a given sentence by the meaning of the sentence. For example, the word *copy* has several definitions, including these two: **1.** to make a copy of. **2.** to imitate.

- Show with a check which definition applies in each sentence below:

    The boy learned to swear by *copying* his father.   1 ___   2 √

    Everyone *copied* the homework assignment into their notebooks.   1 √   2 ___

5. Other Information.   After the definitions in a listing in a hardbound dictionary, you may get brief information about the *origin,* or beginning, of a word. Such information about origins, also known as *etymology,* is usually given in brackets ([ ]). And you may sometimes be given one or more synonyms or antonyms for the entry word. *Synonyms* are words that are similar in meaning to the entry word; *antonyms* are words that are opposite in meaning.

WHICH DICTIONARIES TO OWN

You will find it useful to own two recent dictionaries: a small paperback dictionary to carry to class and a hardbound dictionary, which contains more information than a small paperback one. Among the good dictionaries strongly recommended are both the paperback and hardcover editions of the following:

> *The Random House College Dictionary*
> *The American Heritage Dictionary*
> *Webster's New World Dictionary*

ANSWERS TO THE DICTIONARY QUESTIONS

Guide words: *liquid* / *litter*
Number of syllables: 3, 4, 5
Vowels: *camp, silk* (short); *pie* (long)
Schwa: second syllable of *thunder*

Accent: stronger accent on third syllable
Parts of speech: noun and verb
Definitions: 2; 1

C. Word List

abundant, 97
accompany, 61
accustomed, 125
adequate, 137
advise, 45
aggravate, 89
analyze, 93
anticipate, 101
anxious, 21
apparent, 121
appeal, 65
appropriate, 9
artificial, 105
assume, 53
attitude, 133
automatic, 121
awkward, 137
betray, 117
bewilder, 9
brutal, 129
burden, 13
category, 93
cease, 89
challenge, 73
coincide, 109
communicate, 5
comparison, 117
complicate, 77
comprehend, 25
conflict, 33
conscience, 77
conscious, 49
considerable, 109
contrast, 133
convince, 21
counsel, 77
critical, 93
current, 41

customary, 137
deceive, 5
deliberate, 93
demonstrate, 97
dependent, 81
deprive, 45
desperate, 61
detect, 77
determine, 17
discipline, 129
dispose of, 17
dispute, 117
distinct, 97
dramatic, 25
earnest, 5
economical, 13
eliminate, 129
emotion, 9
emphasis, 69
establish, 65
evident, 17
exaggerate, 97
excessive, 133
exhaust, 53
external, 49
extravagant, 13
fertile, 73
fiction, 5
fragile, 133
frank, 25
frequency, 105
frustration, 93
fulfill, 121
furthermore, 129
hesitate, 45
humane, 89
illustrate, 25
impression, 25

incredible, 49
indicate, 133
inferior, 21
influence, 121
inhabit, 117
intentional, 109
interference, 89
internal, 49
interpret, 69
investigate, 9
legible, 9
linger, 101
maintain, 41
maximum, 53
minimum, 41
miserable, 101
misinterpret, 125
neutral, 117
objection, 45
objective, 53
obnoxious, 89
occur, 125
originate, 41
overwhelm, 21
peculiar, 73
penalize, 45
possess, 37
potential, 65
preference, 81
preserve, 17
principal, 81
procedure, 37
propose, 69
protest, 53
pursue, 61
reduction, 97
rejection, 61
reliable, 41

reluctant, 101
remedy, 49
renew, 37
represent, 105
resort, 129
resource, 37
respond, 137
restore, 17
revise, 125
scarce, 61
security, 13
solitary, 81
specific, 101
stress, 33
sufficient, 37
suitable, 81
surplus, 73
sympathize, 13
temporary, 105
theory, 5
thorough, 21
transfer, 121
transform, 73
transparent, 77
triumph, 10-5
ultimate, 69
unanimous, 33
unstable, 109
utilize, 109
vague, 69
vanish, 137
variety, 65
vary, 33
version, 125
vicinity, 33
wholesome, 65